MODELS OF THE MIND
Their Relationships
to Clinical Work

Workshop Series of the
American Psychoanalytic Association

Monograph 1

MODELS OF THE MIND
Their Relationships
to Clinical Work

Editor

ARNOLD ROTHSTEIN, M.D.

INTERNATIONAL UNIVERSITIES PRESS, INC.

NEW YORK   NEW YORK

Library of Congress Cataloging in Publication Data
Main entry under title:

Models of the mind.

  (Workshop series of the American Psychoanalytic Association; monograph 1)
    Bibliography: p.
    Includes index.
    1. Psychoanalysis—Addresses, essays, lectures.
I. Rothstein, Arnold, 1936–   . II. Series.
RC509.M63   1985   616.89'17   85-10844
ISBN 0-8236-3410-8

Manufactured in the United States of America

Contents

Contributors   vii

Preface   ix

Introduction   1

1   A Historical Review of Psychoanalytic Paradigms
    Arnold M. Cooper, M.D.   5

2   The Structural Hypothesis
    Jacob A. Arlow, M.D.   21

3   The Klein–Bion Model
    Hanna Segal, M.D.   35

4   The Interpersonal (Sullivanian) Model
    Edgar Levenson, M.D.   49

5   Psychoanalytic Self Psychology
    Arnold Goldberg, M.D.   69

6   Object Relations Theory
    Arnold H. Modell, M.D.   85

7   Lacanian Theory
    William J. Richardson, Ph.D.   101

8   A Discussion of the Various Theories
    Joseph Sandler, Ph.D., M.D.   119

9 Conclusion
        Arnold Rothstein, M.D.   129

    Appendix: The Spontaneous Discussion   137
    References   149
    Name Index   153
    Subject Index   155

Contributors

JACOB A. ARLOW, M.D.   Past President, American Psychoanalytic Association; Former Editor-in-Chief, *Psychoanalytic Quarterly*

ARNOLD M. COOPER, M.D.   Professor of Psychiatry and Director of Psychiatric Education, Cornell University Medical College; Supervising and Training Analyst, Columbia University Center for Psychoanalytic Training and Research; Past President, American Psychoanalytic Association

ARNOLD GOLDBERG, M.D.   Training and Supervising Analyst, The Chicago Institute for Psychoanalysis; coauthor, *Models of the Mind*

EDGAR LEVENSON, M.D.   Training and Supervisory Analyst, William Alanson White Institute; Clinical Professor of Psychology, New York University; author, *The Fallacy of Understanding* and *The Ambiguity of Change*

ARNOLD H. MODELL, M.D.   Training and Supervising Analyst, Boston Psychoanalytic Institute; Clinical Professor of Psychiatry, Harvard Medical School; Psychiatrist, Beth Israel Hospital (Boston); author, *Object Love and Reality* and *Psychoanalysis in a New Context*

WILLIAM J. RICHARDSON, Ph.D.   Professor of Philosophy, Boston College; graduate, William Alanson White Institute; coauthor, *Lacan and Language: Reader's Guide to Ecrits*

ARNOLD ROTHSTEIN, M.D.   Faculty, Columbia University Center for Psychoanalytic Training and Research; author, *The Narcissistic Pursuit of Perfection* and *The Structural Hypothesis: An Evolutionary Perspective*

JOSEPH SANDLER, Ph.D., M.D.   Sigmund Freud Professor of Psychoanalysis, the Hebrew University of Jerusalem, and Freud Memorial Professor of Psychoanalysis, University of London

HANNA SEGAL, M.D.   Fellow, Royal College of Psychiatrists, London; Member and Training Analyst of the British Psychoanalytic Society

Preface

The Workshops for Mental Health Professionals were initiated in 1976 by the Program Committee of the American Psychoanalytic Association with the heuristic aim of offering the entire mental health community an exposure to the expertise of Association analysts in regard to fundamental subjects of concern to practitioners in the field. This aim derives from the program committee's wish to reach out to the community at large and encourage both attendance at our national meetings and these workshops. This desire and the derivative policies and programs originate from the concept that psychoanalysis, beyond its immediate therapeutic applications in the specifically psychoanalytic clinical situation, is a general psychology applicable in modified forms to many aspects of other clinical as well as nonclinical endeavors.

Past workshops have explored a number of subjects of basic interest to mental health practitioners: "Specific Problems in the Treatment of Adolescents"; "Specific Problems in Brief Psychotherapy"; "Children's Reactions to Object Loss"; "Special Problems in the Psychotherapy of Depression"; "The Transference in Psychotherapy: Clinical Management"; "The Significance of Infant Observational Research Data for Clinical Work"; "The Relationships of Models of the Mind to Clinical Work"; and "The Significance of the Reconstruction of Trauma in Clinical Work." Future workshops plan to explore "The Significance of Dream Interpretation in Clinical Work" as well as the question of the mode of therapeutic action of psychoanalytic psychotherapy.

The format of the two-day workshops has facilitated an in-depth exploration of one subject and provided ample unstructured time for spontaneous discussion of formal presentations. These discussions have facilitated the clarification and development of participants' contributions.

In response to the high caliber of the learning experience many participants in the workshop have suggested the value of a written record of these proceedings. Toward that end, the Executive Committee of the American Psychoanalytic Association decided to sponsor the development of a series of publications deriving from these educational endeavors. The participants have been able to clarify and develop their ideas further in the process of developing the presentations into written form.

The workshop that resulted in this monograph began with my introductory remarks and Arnold Cooper's paper—both of these presentations provided a facilitating frame of reference for the proponents of the models being considered. The remainder of the first day of the workshop was devoted to two panels chaired by Sydney Pulver and Charles Brenner, at which Jacob Arlow, Hanna Segal, Edgar Levenson, Arnold Goldberg, Arnold Modell, William Richardson presented their models of the mind. The panel, held the second day of the workshop, was entitled "Conversations with the Panelists" and was chaired by Robert Michels. It began with a formal discussion of the previous days presentations by Joseph Sandler. Then all of the participants engaged in an unstructured discussion for three hours about the fundamental questions raised by the workshop. These discussions as well as the spontaneous discussions after each presentation are reported in the appendix.

Arnold Rothstein, M.D.
November 1984

Introduction

Arnold Rothstein, M.D.

Psychoanalytic models have always emerged from the dialectic between clinical experience and the observer –experiencer's need to organize that experience in some abstract conceptual framework. These hypothetical constructs are influenced by the observer's personality as well as by his personal and professional value systems, and by prevailing theories in other disciplines. The first psychoanalytic model emerged from the collaborative efforts of Breuer and Freud. Breuer returned to his medical practice in defensive flight from erotic countertransference. Freud persevered, and through clinical experience and self-analysis, particularly dream analysis, found Breuer's theories, especially the hypnoid model and the actual seduction theory, wanting. Freud discovered infantile sexuality, the Oedipus complex, and transference; he proposed the topographic model of the mind, and described the dreamwork characteristic of the wish-fulfilling function of dreams.

Subsequent clinical experience influenced Freud to emend his model and propose an alternative model, the structural hypothesis, and a corresponding revised theory of anxiety.

Before psychoanalysis was out of its teens, Jung and Adler had questioned some of Freud's hypotheses and emphases. This questioning process regularly resulted in some questioners disassociating themselves from Freud and those of his collaborators who agreed with Freud. These partings were anything but amicable; the dissenters established competing schools of psychoanalysis bearing their names and proposed new models. They were considered courageous, creative innovators by their followers, and misguided, poorly analyzed souls by those Freudians who watched their departure. Communication between differing perspectives has, in general, been difficult. Cooper (1982) noted that in recent psychoanalytic history the participants have been more mature; schisms have been less frequent, and colleagues with radically different points of view have functioned within the same organizations and worked to communicate their ideas to each other. Contributions from related disciplines that describe the process of developments in science have contributed to the maturation of psychoanalysis by providing the discipline with metatheoretical perspectives to facilitate observations of their development.

T.S. Kuhn is one such scholar of the history of science whose influential book *The Structure of Scientific Revolutions* (1962) has had a significant impact on contemporary analytic thought. In it he describes competition in the hard sciences between established science and innovators who challenge the established conception of reality. He suggests that the term *paradigm* or *disciplinary matrix* be defined in both a broad and a narrow sense. In the broad sense, "it stands for the entire constellation of beliefs, values, techniques . . . shared by members of a given community" (p. 175). In the narrow sense, "it denotes one sort of element in that constellation, the concrete puzzle-solutions which, employed as models or examples, can replace explicit rules as a basis for the solution of the remaining puzzles of normal science" (p. 175).

Contemporary mental health practitioners live in a world in which they are confronted by a panoply of paradigms competing for their admiration, allegiance and fealty. In addition to its heuristic purpose the workshop was organized in order to explore some of the implications of this state of affairs. Toward that end six analysts associated with particular theoretical perspectives were asked to define their paradigms in the broad and narrow sense and to present clinical data organized within the constructs they espouse. They were sent these introductory remarks five months prior to the workshop to facilitate their thinking about the task. Dr. Arnold Cooper was invited to present a history of the development of psychoanalytic models of the mind in order to provide a framework for the ensuing discussions. The panelists were informed that their panels would be chaired by eminent colleagues, Drs. Charles Brenner, Robert Michels, and Sydney Pulver, and thus were assured that the American Psychoanalytic Association was doing everything in its power to create an ambiance in which various proponents could compete and attempt to communicate across the tangible boundaries that their models had contributed to creating. In addition they were informed that Dr. Joseph Sandler would formally discuss all the presentations within the format of the final panel "Conversations with the Panelists," in which the entire faculty of the workshop would participate. The organization of this final panel provided three hours of unstructured time for more spontaneous discussion emphasizing the program committee's fundamental commitment to the facilitation of communication. In that regard I concluded these introductory remarks by raising a number of questions concerning the possible future process of developments in psychoanalysis to be considered during the final panel. How can communication across paradigms be facilitated? What role can research play in answering questions raised by different points of view? What kinds of research strategies are appropriate to psychoanalysis?

Chapter 1

A Historical Review of Psychoanalytic Paradigms

Arnold M. Cooper, M.D.

Philosophers of science agree that all pursuit of knowledge, scientific or otherwise, is highly determined by the underlying theories that the investigator holds of the universe he is observing. Without a theory, we are unable to select data from the massive jumble of impressions that constantly assail us. Neither psychoanalysts nor naive psychologists—the man in the street—are able to function without a theory. It is desirable, however, for the psychoanalyst to know what his theory is, since it will determine important actions he takes in the course of his work. The purpose of this book is to help us know which theories we hold and to try to understand the consequences of those theories for our clinical activity.

Our psychoanalytic literature has maintained that there is a close relationship between psychoanalytic theory and psychoanalytic practice. However, since psychoanalytic theory has often been elaborated at high levels of abstraction, that unity of theory and practice may not always be as clear as we would wish. Theories that lack significant consequences for clinical work may be interesting for other purposes, but clearly cannot be held to be clinically valuable. It seems to be a characteristic of complex fields—cosmology, evolution, social science, psychology—that large and overarching theories are constructed in an attempt to provide guidance and justification for the investigator in what may otherwise be a disorganized terrain. These theories usually include within them an attempt to imagine back to first causes; an effort to understand the moment of creation, as it were, in order to unify all subsequent observation. In psychoanalysis, the effort to construct those experience-distant theories, the metapsychology of psychoanalysis, has often seemed excessively remote from the activities of data collection and organization; so much so that the late George Klein once suggested that we call a moratorium on theorizing and try instead to discover the nature of our clinical data. Of course, we cannot call a moratorium on theorizing, but we can examine the effects of our ideas on our clinical behavior.

While the title of this chapter is "A Historical Review of Psychoanalytic Paradigms," I would like to revise that title and suggest that we should talk about psychoanalytic theories or ideas. The term *paradigm*, as developed by Kuhn, refers to a core conception around which new data accumulates. It seems to me not to apply to the many revisions of Freud's theory that have been suggested over the last three-quarters of a century, some of which will be discussed in this book. I think that Freud was the only true revolutionary, and other psychoanalysts, no matter how non-Freudian or anti-Freudian, have been playing variations on the themes Freud established. The paradigm Freud constructed, in grossly oversimplified form, consisted of a claim of psychic determinism; a method of investigation—free association; a descriptive-explanatory proposition that behavior is influenced or determined by powerful feelings and ideas occurring out of awareness—the dynamic unconscious; and a treatment method based on the recognition of the central role of transference. It is my suggestion that these core ideas form the agreed upon base for any set of propositions that should go by the title, "Psychoanalysis." While one or another school has from time to time claimed that theirs is a new psychoanalytic paradigm, and perhaps in the narrow sense of the term that is correct, I think it best to put that issue aside as we try to scan the shifts in theoretical stance and the new ideas on the relationships of the models of the mind to clinical work.

The depth psychology which Freud both discovered and invented, and which generally goes by the name of psychoanalysis, has enjoyed its enormous success as an explanatory system because its few basic propositions are open to endless elaboration, revision, and refinement; and because the special investigative mode of communicated introspection in the transference relationship produces a unique knowledge of the mind. Rather quickly after he began his investigations, Freud developed a relatively simple description of human behavior as having dynamic, economic, and topographic qualities. He believed that any interesting human act could be understood if we knew three things: first, the nature of the mental forces contending for control of access to action (the dynamic proposition); second, the relative strengths of these forces; and third, a delineation of which of these forces, experienced as ideas and feelings, were conscious and which were not. But even as Freud was making his clinical discoveries and putting them into the form of descriptive propositions, he was already at work on his Project; an early effort to place his clinical discoveries in a larger neurophysiologic theoretical framework from which the clinical data would be derivative. I will not recount here the development of Freud's metapsychology, but I do want to emphasize the enormous importance to psychoanalysis of Freud's attitudes toward his theories and discoveries. In 1925a, Freud was able to say of his topographic scheme, "Such ideas as these are part of a speculative superstructure of psychoanalysis, any portion of which can be abandoned or changed without loss or regret the moment its inadequacy has been proved" (p. 33). In fact, he did change his theories often and radically in response to new insights. In a famous passage in 1937 he referred to his theoretical superstructure as "The Witch Metapsychology. Without metapsychological speculation and theorizing—I have almost said fantasying—we shall not get another step forward. Unfortunately, here as elsewhere, what our Witch reveals is neither very clear nor very detailed" (p. 225). Freud knew full well the difference between his dispensable theories and his core findings. It would, however, be terribly misleading if we were to think that Freud held his theories lightly. While he showed an extraordinary theoretical flexibility himself, he was almost equally intolerant of theoretical deviation by others, and even resented theoretical inventiveness among his own follow- ers. The unfortunate episode with Tausk, Freud's stated aim of having the International Psychoanalytic Association serve as a central clearinghouse for ideas so that they could be con- formed with analytic doctrine before being given a public hear- ing, and his relations with his followers, were indications of his need, personally, to create the major theories. These tendencies of Freud assured the orderly development of certain aspects of psychoanalysis, but forced other important ideas into op- positional schools or onto sidetracks where they could not in- teract with the main directions of psychoanalytic development. This situation has changed only recently—a book such as this one would have been inconceivable only a decade ago.

Furthermore, it is important to note that Freud, while clear at certain periods about the dispensable and indispensable as- pects of this theory, at other times defended most ferociously parts of the theory which were surely not the unalterable core of psychoanalysis, but data-dependent propositions which could be revised without any damage to the integrity of the psychoan- alytic theoretical structure. Questions of the nuclear role of the Oedipus complex in neurosogenesis, or of the centrality of energic propositions for psychoanalytic explanation, would be examples of this.

The *indispensable* core of psychoanalysis has always con- sisted of a very few propositions, to which I alluded earlier, and which remain constant through the various changes and shifts of Freud's thinking. Psychic determinism refers to the concept that psychological actions have psychological causes and that those causes can be studied. The concept of psychic determin- ism is essential, since the alternative is a random series of events not amenable to scientific explanation. Implied in the concept of psychic determination is a system of motivation. Freud's

motivational system is based on the pleasure–unpleasure principle; behavior is understood as the adaptive effort to maximize
experiences of pleasure and escape from unpleasure. Furthermore, the origins of behavior lie, at least in part, in the biological
nature of the organism itself and are not simply responses to
stimuli from the outside world; the organism is driven. Another
core concept, the genetic–developmental proposition, also derives from the concept of psychic determinism, and states that
all behavior is understood as a sequence of behaviors developing
out of earliest infantile events. And finally, the concept of the
dynamic unconscious, which I have described earlier, is a core
proposition.

Attached to this theoretical core are two propositions I have
already mentioned that form the clinical core of psychoanalysis.
These are communicated introspection through free association; and the phenomenon of transference in the patient –
therapist interaction.

I would like now to describe in a very brief form a few of
the major shifts in Freud's own thinking. I will then go on to
mention a few of the major theoretical schools which arose as
deviations from, or in opposition to, Freud's thought, and will
then discuss some of the enduring ambiguities and points of
contention that have emerged as long-standing differences
among psychoanalysts, and have been a stimulus for new ideas
or schools.

Freud initially believed that he had discovered the etiology
of neurosis in the actual event of childhood sexual seduction.
In this conception, an interpersonal event was the trauma that
led to the unresolved conflict expressed in the compromise of
the symptom. The subsequent abandonment of the seduction
hypothesis, which I believe was an essential step for the development of psychoanalysis rather than social theory, led to a
focus on fantasy and on the sources of fantasy in instinct or
drive.

This second theory, emphasizing fantasy, effectively removed social interaction from the center of analytic thought,

and led to an attempt to understand all actions as ultimately stemming from biologically based sexual drives. A third major shift occurred with the creation of the dual instinct theory, giving equal weight to aggression and sexuality, and with the revised theory of anxiety, which placed the perception of danger in the center of analytic attention. A danger situation was specified as the fear of helplessness resulting from loss—the loss of mother, the loss of mother's love, the loss of the penis, or the loss of the superego's love. This third theoretical revision restored interaction with, and adaptation to, the real world as an essential part of psychoanalytic explanation.

Finally, there is the invention of the structural schema of ego, id, and superego, a hypothesis which has had extraordinary explanatory power and which led eventually to an emphasis on the centrality of the ego's executive role, both in providing the signal of anxiety and in constructing the defenses which organize the characterologic and symptomatic constructions of ongoing individual life. This shift from id analysis toward ego analysis was strongly assisted by Anna Freud and Hartmann.

All of these changes and advances in psychoanalytic thinking were parts of what Freud referred to as the metapsychological, that is, the *dispensable* aspect of theoretical explanation. This is not to gainsay their importance in leading us to new data and clinical advances.

While Freud, in a way, saw everything, it is clear that he had biases and predilections which made it difficult for him to give evenhanded attention to matters that today seem of major importance. I refer to such ideas as the developmental significance of the real role of real parents and the culture they represent; the significance of preoedipal events; the role of dependency, attachment, and safety in development alongside the role of instinctual drives; the central organizing and synthesizing functions of an ego or self; and the importance of nonconflictual aspects of development, to mention but a few. These, and other areas of Freud's opposition or inattention have been the gaps in the standard theory which many of the alternate or revised psychoanalytic theories have attempted to fill.

A portion of the growth of psychoanalytic theory can be seen as the effort to incorporate, often without acknowledgement, the valid aspects of the critique of oppositional schools. Recently, for example, Sullivan's work has increasingly reappeared in mainstream psychoanalysis, not always with attribution.

The first serious challenges to Freud's psychoanalysis came from Jung and Adler (whose theories are not discussed in this work). Putting aside all of the fascinating data concerning the personal relationship of Freud and Jung, their disagreement was theoretically profound from the start, and Jung was never able to accept either the central role of sexuality in Freud's thought or the concept of mechanism. Jung insisted on a more magical and mystical mode of explanation. However, his critique of libido theory and his focus on a central role for some version of self-concept were important determiners in Freud's struggle with issues of narcissism, and played a part in the gradual rise of ego psychology.

Adler founded his school of individual psychology because of his conviction that the central motivator for human action was the drive for superiority or mastery or assertion. Freud responded to Adler's deviation by condemning Adler's abandonment of psychoanalysis, but Freud eventually found the way to introduce aggression into his own theoretical framework.

Finally, I will mention Otto Rank, whose theory of the birth trauma emphasized issues of loss and merging as the original sources of anxiety. Again, Freud, convinced by Abraham that Rank had to be abandoned, eventually revised his own theory of anxiety to take into account the very issues which Rank had raised.

These major figures founded schools or movements which survive today. Rank was a powerful influence on the social work movement in the United States and can properly be considered the father of brief, time-limited focal psychotherapy. Some

Jungian theorists believe that if one strips the mysticism from Jung one can see Jung's current relevance as a leader both in understanding issues of narcissism and in pointing to the importance of ongoing developmental changes throughout the life cycle.

Existential analysis is another psychoanalytic school of thought which has been influential, and is also not represented in this book. The effort of the existentialists has been to bring psychoanalysis back to the phenomenologic core of the interaction of the persons involved in the analytic process and the description of their direct experience. In the view of the existentialists, Freud's love affair with his metapsychology and with nineteenth century scientific ideas of causality had led to the errors of reductionism and mechanization. Clearly, those currently interested in hermeneutic propositions in analysis share a similar view.

It is my suggestion that Freud's protectiveness of his ideas and his belief that the development of psychoanalysis would best be served by founding a movement rather than a forum for open scientific discussion of competing ideas, while probably essential for the rapid triumph of psychoanalysis within western culture, also contributed to the sectarianism of early psychoanalytic thought and the tendency for each new system to attempt completion and closure. It is significant that after the early splits with Jung, Adler, and Rank, psychoanalysts with different or opposing ideas, especially in Europe, tended to "bore from within," managing to remain a part of mainstream psychoanalysis and gradually exerting a powerful influence. Klein, Fairbairn, and Winnicott fall into this category as do Kohut, Rado, and Kardiner in America. The gradual maturation of psychoanalytic thought and the psychoanalytic movement has led to a diminution of fear and cultism, the willingness to give up shibboleths, and to renewed attempts to look to our clinical experience and to the data from adjacent sciences, such as infant observation or linguistics, for assistance in understanding what we think about and how we should act therapeutically. Psychoanalysis is open today in a way that it never was before. The change is particularly apparent in America. In Europe, Kleinian and other object-relational approaches have coexisted with ego psychology for decades. In America, the successes of the ego psychological point of view have largely excluded other points of view until very recently.

Many factors have contributed to the change in psychoanalysis toward scientific openness. The widespread basic acceptance of psychoanalysis in the general culture and the profound interest in psychoanalysis in academia have led to psychoanalytic theorizing by theologians, philosophers, neurobiologists, historians, anthropologists, literary critics, and others. No one can control the flow of ideas any longer, and ideas from outside the fold cannot be dismissed. The perceived change in the patient population, with an alleged increase in narcissistic pathology, not easily treatable by standard methods; the awareness of frequent therapeutic failures; the increasing length of analysis; the changing views of science; and the change of authority relations in our society which subtly influence the doctor–patient relationship; have all contributed toward a loosening of once firmly held psychoanalytic belief systems and to the competition of ideas in the field.

I would like now to outline a few of the enduring conceptual disputes in psychoanalysis around which schools of thought and modes of practice have tended to cluster.

Freud at one time said that belief in the Oedipus complex as the nucleus of neurosis is a shibboleth separating analysts from nonanalysts. I (1983) have elsewhere delineated Freud's own later ambivalence toward this pronouncement. However, the issue of the central role of the Oedipus complex is a continuing source of lively debate. It is central for Kleinian theorists, self psychologists, and at least some object-relational psychoanalysts to maintain that the crucial events of neurosogenesis are preoedipal in nature and are reconstructible within the psychoanalytic situation. This is an instance of an important debate which, it seems, could be refereed by the accumulation of clinical data. So far, however, the same clinical data are used by the opposing theorists to prove their different views, a matter to which I will return. The issue of Oedipal or preoedipal etiology is an important one since it shifts the focus in our understanding of etiologic events of neurosis and character pathology and changes our clinical interventions in the psychoanalytic situation.

A second issue concerns the significance—even the psychic reality—of the actual environment of maturation and development. The classical psychoanalytic view has emphasized the genetic viewpoint, which focuses on the intrapsychic experience of the world and is relatively uninterested in the actual world in which that intrapsychic experience developed. There is a subtle assumption that the maturational stages of drives will have a more dominant effect on outcome than the accidents of environment. In contrast, the developmental view, essential for Kohut and Sullivan, important for Winnicott, posits that the *actual* behaviors of the mother are a determining part of the infant's experience; and furthermore that the infant is a more or less accurate registrar of the mother, and the infantile experience is recoverable in analysis. Data from infant psychiatry research heavily support the significance attributed to the beneficent or malevolent influences of the real mother in shaping development. However, the counterargument of adult analysts is that while that data is relevant for child rearing, it is irrelevant for the conduct of psychoanalysis, since in analysis we have available only the reconstructed narrative of the patient in the analytic situation. That reconstruction has little or no truth value, nor is the issue of truth relevant for analytic purposes. What the patient internalized is what the situation was.

A third significant discussion concerns the nature of the unit studied in psychoanalysis. Is the unit of study an individual, or an interaction? Sullivan, some of the object relations theorists, and Kohut, at times, have insisted that the appropriate unit is, at the least, an infant–parent dyad, and that, in fact, we have no way to conceive of the infant apart from the tie to the parent. For Sullivan the self is constructed out of the reflections of one's self received from others. Kohut, somewhat less radically, conceives a biologically developing self powerfully influenced by the actions of others. On the other hand, Kohut approaches the interpersonal point of view in his conception of the individual as "living in a sea of self-objects," and always requiring actual objects for the maintenance of internalized self-objects, without which the self shrivels.

A fourth issue concerns the varying prescriptions for the proper behavior of the therapist in the therapeutic situation. Freud suggested that the analyst should maintain a neutrality similar to that of a surgeon who must inflict pain on his patient, and the analyst should be a reflecting mirror in which the patient may see himself. At the same time, we know from numerous descriptions of Freud with his patients that he was able to act spontaneously, and even idiosyncratically, in ways that we would never tolerate today. Freud seemed to take for granted that the analyst behaved humanely and decently, with little concern for any disruptive effects on the treatment due to the analyst's behavior. All the available evidence indicates that Freud himself was at a rather far remove from the model of the silent analyst creating a climate of libidinal abstinence, which some have taken as the classical analytic stance. Questions of the meaning and role of empathic responsiveness, or the holding environment, or technical neutrality, or the analyst as screen, are not new. Ferenczi and Rank, in 1922, were critical of the silent analyst. Fairbairn (1952), at the end of his career, abandoned the use of the couch, which he likened to placing an infant in a crib which prevented his seeing his parents; he believed this was a setting of cruelty, not neutrality.

This issue of the proper stance of the analyst relates to another long-standing question concerning the role of the analyst as a real person in the here-and-now treatment situation, influencing the manifestations of the transference. Is transference interactive, or is it a private fantasy of the patient imposed upon the neutral analyst? Furthermore, is the significant treatment event the reconstruction of the past out of which the transference has been created, or is it the affective experience in the current relationship to the analyst? Clearly, interpersonal analysts, joined by self psychologists, Merton Gill, and others, will view these matters differently from analysts following what until recently was assumed to be Freud's standard technique.

Yet another long-lasting debate concerns the basic constitution of the human nature which different theories describe. Freud's infant and adult is, by nature's design, in opposition to an environment which must tame and inhibit his pleasures. Instinct and society are, of necessity, in conflict; ambivalence is the norm and conflict is inevitable. In sharpest contrast, Kohut's infant and, I suspect Jung's and Sullivan's, are, by their nature, potentially consonant with their environment, provided the environment does not fail them through malevolence or unresponsiveness. Clearly, one's view on whether or not the individual is seen as inevitably conflicted and ambivalent, or potentially harmonious in his quest for self-realization—Freud's guilty man in contrast to Kohut's tragic man—will powerfully influence the content and timing of interpretations. In fact, the entire goal of psychoanalysis will vary with one's views on this issue.

I will briefly allude to only a few more such divisions within psychoanalysis. The question of whether psychoanalysis is, by its nature, a hermeneutic discipline; that is, a purely psychological and linguistic effort at understanding meanings, or whether it is a scientific causal discipline with biological roots, is seriously debated today. Here, Lacan, Kohut, and Schafer would part from ego-psychological views. Implied in much of what I have already said, is the complex ongoing discussion over what in psychoanalysis is the therapeutic element—the interpretation, the empathic experience, the holding environment, the regressive opportunity for new growth, and so on.

In all of these debates the sides have not remained static. All of psychoanalysis has been affected by the perception that our patient population has undergone a profound change from neurotic to characterologic. Whether the patients have changed or whether we have changed, the resulting need for newer, creative solutions to clinical problems has contributed to the more open climate of psychoanalytic discussion and to the subtle but important changes in the theory and practice of all parties. We have increasingly heard and learned from each other, and, I suspect, that while our debates remain sharp, our best practice is more alike than it used to be; an indication either that aspects of our clinical work are not explained by our theory or that dearly held theories are irrelevant for clinical work.

During the past several years there has been a definite shift in psychoanalytic interest toward a clarification of what it is that we actually do in psychoanalysis, rather than how we think about what we think we do. American Psychoanalytic Association panels on the clinical consequences of different models of the mind, the International Psychoanalytic Association conference in July 1983 on "The Analyst at Work," and the present volume, are part of the trend. This return to the clinical core of psychoanalysis will, if carried out diligently, lead to new and better and more productive theoretical constructions, which will, in turn, inform our clinical work.

I will now briefly discuss some of the characteristics of models of the mind, suggesting a model of models.

Each creator of a model is trying to offer an explanation of a puzzling characteristic of human behavior. (Clearly each investigator finds his puzzle out of his own psychological makeup; it is an important aspect of psychoanalysis that all theories are subject to psychoanalytic understanding and reconstruction. Any product of the human mind can be scrutinized psychoanalytically, but that understanding does not affect the scientific validity of the model that has been constructed.) Having identified his problem, each theorist looks to first causes: where in earliest development did this problem appear, either as a part of normal infancy or as a result of infantile trauma, deprivation, or constitutional error. Having identified a first cause, the theorist then looks to its effects on development and to the defensive modes it excites. Each theorist then expands his puzzle solution into a theory for the entirety of the mind. Finally, a logical method of undoing the pathology is suggested, usually involving both a therapeutic attitude and a direction of interpretation.

For example, if one thinks of Sullivan as focusing on problems of alienation and anomie as a core problem of human living, one can observe that he then postulated infantile anxiety, arising as a contagion from the mother, as a first cause. It would then be reasonable that from that first cause an interpersonal theory and technique would be constructed in the effort to solve the problem. Similarly, if one conceives of observing inauthenticity and the false self as the core problem, one finds the first cause as a failure of good enough mothering, and the solution in a provision of a holding environment. Again, one can see Kohut's core puzzle as a question of how one develops an enfeebled self, and his postulated first cause as the mother's failure of empathic responsiveness. In helping to build a self, the remedy then lies in a repair of self-object ties through the provision of the previously missing empathic responsiveness. Melanie Klein, interested in primitive childhood thinking, postulates forms of an infantile psychotic core which gains dynamic power because of faulty internalizations. The solution lies in direct cognitive interpretation of the psychotic reenactments of the transference.

Further, as we read the literature of each school, it becomes clear that each theorist tends to see the patients that fit the theory, or perhaps they reconstruct their patients in ways that fit the theory. For example, it seems clear that Kleinian psychoanalysts see a much sicker population than the ego psychologists.

One can follow this exercise in models further and demonstrate that each school is attempting to deal with a *specific* human problem and then broadens its scope to include the full spectrum of human behavior. It would be my suggestion that the core of Freud's model, to which I alluded earlier, is the only model that provides for that full spectrum of human behavior, while the others provide for special, although often important variants.

One of the issues to be raised concerns the question of specificity of treatment. Are different schools designed for the treatment of different kinds of patients, or does each have a technique that treats everyone? In an earlier paper (unpublished), I have suggested that our current theoretical plurality provides an excellent opportunity to test the efficacy of different treatments. To my surprise, theorists of very different persuasions quickly united to say that they were all doing the same psychoanalysis, only each was doing it a little better. We should take the opportunity of this competition of theories to emphasize the *differences* in clinical work; not for the sake of argument, but because only by understanding our differences can we begin to test different treatment methods, expose to public scrutiny what we actually do, and hope to learn to do it better.

Finally, a word of caution: Our theoretical and clinical debates are likely to be long lasting. It is, fortunately for our patients, but unfortunately for research, the case that psychoanalysis cannot be conducted with an as-if attitude. If we do not believe in our theories and techniques, then we cannot conduct the experiment which would allow us to determine their truth or falsity. For example, Kohut recommends for certain narcissistic patients a long noninterpretive period at the beginning of the analysis. Without, at least, a very sympathetic view of Kohut's theories, it is not possible to maintain a noninterpretive stance for several years in the face of the patient's regression, aggressions, idealizations, denigrations, and so on. The work of analysis is too taxing for us to attempt a stance we do not believe in; furthermore, our patients quickly catch on if we are faking it. In science, we are dependent on the replication of reports by different scientists in different laboratories. Unfortunately, in psychoanalysis, we cannot replicate the experimental setting, since we are, ourselves, the major portion of the experimental apparatus as well as the experimenter. We neither duplicate easily, nor can we be blind to our own activity. The problem of validation is a serious one and will require that we all cooperate if we are to produce new clinical data and learn new methods.

Chapter 2

The Structural Hypothesis

Jacob A. Arlow, M.D.

In the course of his clinical work, the analyst is profoundly influenced by the model of the mind to which he subscribes. While he may not be aware of this at all times, his theory of mental functioning constantly guides what he says and what he does. It influences how he attends to what the patient is saying, what he perceives in the patient's productions, and how he organizes his observations.

The structural hypothesis represents an organic development from the fundamental postulates of psychoanalysis. The concepts that make up the foundations of psychoanalysis are psychic determinism, dynamic conflict (the interplay of opposing trends or impulses), and unconscious mental processes. For me, the idea that intrapsychic conflict is the basic dimension of mental functioning in general and of psychopathology in particular is inexorable and unequivocal. The cumulative observations of almost 100 years of psychoanalytic experience confirm this. The nature of our investigative instrument, the psychoanalytic situation, articulates it. In fact, as Freud described in his "An Autobiographical Study" (1925), the psychoanalytic situation and its quintessential component, free association, were designed to facilitate the emergence into consciousness of derivatives of persistent unconscious conflicts. In describing his turn to free associations, Freud said, "Hypnosis had screened from view *an interplay of forces* which now came in sight and the understanding of which gave a solid foundation to my theory" (p. 29, author's emphasis). The dynamic principle in psychoanalysis is a parallel expression of this interplay in forces, the concept of mental conflict. In the vicissitudes of human experience and development, conflict is an unfailing attribute.

Structural theory was devised precisely for the purpose of organizing and clarifying the phenomenology of mental life as consequences of conflict. The decisive criterion by which each mental element is assigned its place in mental structure is the role that it plays in conflict. The more intense the conflict, the clearer the delineation among the various structures of the mind (A. Freud, 1936). When the ego acts as the executant, harmonizing and integrating the demands of the id and the superego, it is difficult indeed to delineate the boundaries of psychic structure. In any event, considerations of conflict were what led Freud to reformulate his theory of mental functioning in terms of the structural hypothesis and, to my way of thinking, this theory remains the best model, the most effective and comprehensive theory by which one may conceptualize the phenomenology of mental activity.

Within the psychoanalytic situation, free associations offer a living record of the moment to moment functioning of the patient's mind. It is not a placid, continuous scroll of recollections. It is a dynamic record, reflecting a relatively unstable equilibrium of forces in conflict. The phenomenology of this instability is rich and varied, and its dynamism and significance can be grasped in their fullness during the psychoanalytic situation, as one observes and studies the moment to moment variation in the patient's communications. The patient's productions reflect the changing contribution emanating from the several psychic agencies, and they encompass the well-recognized phenomena ordinarily described under the heading of resistance and defense, as well as intrusive fantasies, impulses, thoughts, affective states, parapraxes, and so forth.

The interplay of the forces in conflict determines the form and sequence in which the elements of communication appear in the course of free association. Accordingly, from the patterns that the elements communicated assume, meanings beyond those conveyed in the literal, expository prose can be inferred. Such inferences articulate motives and wishes quite unknown to the analysand, as well as the methods and reasons for disowning and denying such wishes and impulses.

As in any conversation, precision of comprehension depends upon the context, sequence, and contiguity of the ideas presented. Context makes it possible to understand the flow of thoughts, even when one or another element may have been omitted or not heard in the course of the conversation (Rosen, 1967). The contiguity or the juxtaposition of ideas usually means that somehow the elements are semantically related, very much in the way that one word following another gives meaning to a sentence, and one sentence following another gives meaning to a paragraph. In fact, one of the ways of dramatizing our understanding of the nature of the psychoanalytic process is to view it as corresponding to the record of an internal conversation. Although the phrase *internal dialogue* has often been used, it is not sufficiently precise, because the inner argument advances through several protagonists. Many voices are involved and each expresses a different representative of the conflicting forces at work; for example, the pressure of the impulses, warnings, prohibitions, and threats, judgments drawn from experience, and so on. All of these so-called inner voices represent contributions from the events of various periods in the individual's past, interactions with important persons who helped mold character and ideals, as well as the effects of the vicissitudes of individual experience and learning. Under different circumstances and in different situations, regrouping of these voices, or forces, takes place. The participants in the conversation ally themselves at different times and for different reasons with one or another of the protagonists of the inner conflict.

We know from clinical experience how exquisitely this state of affairs may be reproduced in dreams. In some dreams it is possible to demonstrate how each character represents a thought or attitude that is part of the ongoing argument in the psyche. In the psychoanalytic situation, the analyst is privy to this internal argument, to its rich details, and to its historical development. Technique consists of intervening from time to time to make sure that each voice is heard, that each one of the protagonists in the inner debate has his say in turn and does not overwhelm and totally obscure the other participants. By avoiding the role of being a pleader or defender of any of the participants in the argument, the analyst fulfills Anna Freud's (1936) advice that the technical position of the analyst should be equidistant from all of the psychic agencies—the id, ego, superego.

The purpose of this quasi-parable is to illustrate the principle that the structures of the mind, as organized around the concept of the role each one plays in intrapsychic conflict, do indeed reflect and specify some aspect of the functioning of the psyche of a person, the analysand. As a set of hypotheses, the agencies of the mind in structural theory summarize and bring into meaningful relationship, in the most parsimonious way, the clinical observations concerning the vicissitudes of the patient's conflicts, as revealed in the psychoanalytic setting. What the psychoanalytic situation does is to make it possible for the analyst to observe how the dynamic equilibrium in the mind shifts and changes under the influence of current experience, the transference, and, above all, as a result of the analyst's interventions and interpretations. In order to bring the nature of the conflict into consciousness, the analyst intervenes in such a way as to shift the dynamic equilibrium in favor of one or another of the forces in conflict. How the patient attempts to reestablish the equilibrium during the course of treatment, that is, in response to the analyst's interventions, often replicates the vicissitudes of the process of pathogenesis. Thus, any interpretation on the part of the analyst should be regarded as an intervention that tends to destabilize the dynamic equilibrium which the ego struggles to maintain. From the vantage point of psychoanalytic technique, this means that the analyst should concentrate on the dynamic effect his intervention produces, rather than on whether the patient accepts or rejects the interpretation. This is a subject that should receive full treatment in connection with the analysis of defense.

Because of the effect of the interplay of opposing forces in the mind, what finally appears in consciousness represents a compromise formation. Toward this compromise formation each of the various agencies of the mind—the ego, the superego, and the id—has made its specific contribution. From our clinical work we learn to appreciate that what appears in consciousness is a derivative of an unconscious conflict. In two papers (Arlow, 1969a, 1969b), I have called attention to the fact that, at a certain level, the ego's attempt to resolve fundamental, recurrent intrapsychic conflicts is organized in the form of an unconscious fantasy. Essentially, the interpretive work during psychoanalysis consists of reconstructing the nature of the unconscious fantasy from the derivatives which it produces in consciousness, and analyzing and resolving the consequences of the specific component contributions of the forces in conflict. Sometimes the question is raised by those apparently influenced by the topographic model: Where is the unconscious fantasy located? To what system does it belong? Is it part of the ego, the id, or the superego? Actually the situation is the other way around. The id, the ego, and the superego, or, to be more precise, representatives of their influence, are to be found in the unconscious fantasy.

What has been presented thus far is a brief description of the relationship of the structural hypothesis to clinical work. The rich implications of the relationship between this theory of mind and our therapeutic efforts emerge most clearly from a detailed critical examination of the psychoanalytic process over a period of time. In this chapter considerations of space and confidentiality influence me to present a relatively small segment of analytic work to demonstrate the value of the structural model in facilitating the integration and clarification of the meaning of the data of psychoanalytic observation.

This material is from the analysis of a businessman in his forties, who entered treatment for overeating and inability to control his drinking and smoking. Outstanding among the presenting symptoms were feelings of depression and inferiority. The material to be presented centers about the patient's relationship with his older brother, his only sibling, who is nine years his senior. From childhood on, the patient idealized his brother, as well as his brother's friends. Throughout his life the patient would attach himself to older, powerful male figures whom he admired. His relationship to them was that of a mascot. As a mascot he was privy to the activities of the older men and by watching carefully and taking in what he observed, he was able to acquire much of their knowledge and skills. The patient is short of stature and has always been quite insecure about his masculinity. In the period that antedates the material to be described, he became acutely aware of his feelings of phallic inferiority.

The material to be described represents the events of two sessions just before the summer vacation. At the time the patient had reason to be concerned about his brother's health.

The patient began the session by discussing one of his employees, whom he was about to fire. She was not keen about the job because she wanted to go into another business. She was not a reliable person. She had been in psychiatric treatment for a long time, and at the present time was involved in a dispute with her therapist. Because of this dispute she felt that she had a right not to pay the bill. She had left a previous psychiatrist without paying his bill also.

The patient then reported that his brother seemed to be doing better, and went on to discuss how anxious he had been and how reassuring the doctors were when he spoke to them.

The patient's next association was a dream, which follows: "I dreamed I was holding an old style pocket watch in my hand. It had a chain. I was dressed in an old-fashioned suit with a vest, and I was trying to put the watch into my pocket. I was having a great deal of difficulty doing so. There were two intertwined padlocks on the chain, and this made it difficult for me to get the watch into my pocket. Finally it seemed like someone or some force unseen by me was pulling the chain and watch away from me, but I kept holding on to it, determined to keep possession of it. Then I woke up."

The patient said he had never had such a watch. But he then recalled that his father had owned one, and, in fact, his father had worn the kind of clothes that the patient had been wearing in the dream. Actually, he did not have any suits with vests. His father was a dandy; he used to spend a great deal of money on clothes and had bought himself that onion-type watch. The patient then said that he did not know where the watch was. But he corrected himself almost immediately. "Of course I know where the watch is. My brother has it. What happened was that at the time of my father's death six years ago, my mother divided his personal belongings. She asked my older brother if there was anything in particular that he wanted and he said all that he wanted was the watch." The patient said, "I never wanted the watch." "Oh," he said, "that wasn't true. I did want the watch, but not for myself. When my older daughter turned 21, I thought it would be a proper gift to give her now that she had attained her status as an adult. It occurred to me that I would like to get that watch as a gift for her. I thought about it for a while and then decided that I would not ask my brother for it. There was a wristwatch that belonged to my father and I thought I would take it, but before I could say anything, my mother said that she would take the wristwatch."

I pointed out to the patient that in the dream he finally did get possession of the watch. He protested, "No, I never wanted that watch for myself, but I did have it in the dream and I wanted to put it in my pocket, but I couldn't. But I had the watch. My brother got the watch when my father died. How did I get the watch in the dream?" After a pause, he looked up and said, "Is it possible that I inherited the watch from my brother? But that would be ridiculous. One of his children would have gotten it." I observed to him that he had the dream at a time when he felt his brother was safely out of danger.

He then added that he was puzzled by the interlocking of the padlocks that made it impossible for him to get the watch into his own pocket. Padlocks were something you put on the door to prevent the house from being burglarized. A small boat he owned had been stolen recently and since that time he had put such padlocks on his new boat. In any event, the patient went on to add, in the dream he could not enjoy possession of the watch because someone or something was taking it away from him and he could not get it into his pocket. "In the end," he said, "I didn't have the watch, but I didn't let go of it either." He added that his father had been especially proud of that watch. The patient recognized that the watch is a symbol of authority, the kind of heirloom that is passed down through the generations.

At the following session, the patient reported that his brother was not doing as well as previously. He elaborated his concern in some detail. He hoped that in time there would be improvement, but he expressed some doubts.

The patient then reported that he had mentioned the dream of the watch to his wife, as if it were an amusing experience. "Of course," he said, "I omitted any reference to the fact that one of my associations was that I had inherited the watch as a result of my brother's death." His wife pointed out to him that he must have had some need to have the watch for himself, because she knew the watch he was referring to and it would have been a most inappropriate gift for their daughter. It was much too bulky to hang around a woman's neck. The patient responded by saying that this was exactly what he had learned in the session. It was so obvious now that he had used the occasion of his daughter's birthday as an opportunity to express the wish to get the watch for himself. He must have wanted it all the time.

Without transition, the patient said that this reminded him of his father's clothes. "My mother gave me my father's shirts and some other items of apparel after my father died. I have the shirts at home, as well as in my summer place. I have had them now for six years and I have never worn them. I give all sorts of reasons why I don't wear them, but they are not very good reasons. For example, even if they didn't fit well, I could wear them up in my summer place. It wouldn't make any difference there. Everybody dresses informally. I could also wear them around the garden. The same is true of those shirts of my father's that I'm keeping at home. It's also true about the suits that I have of my father's, I can neither wear them nor can I discard them. On several occasions I thought of getting rid of them, of giving them away, but somehow or other, I can't seem to do this."

The observation was made that both the watch and clothes are items that one wears and one is seen wearing. To this, the patient responded, "Oh, but I never connected the watch with the shirts." When I pointed out to the patient that this was exactly what he had just done, he thought for a second and began to laugh. It was all so obvious. He had been talking about the watch and then, without transition, ideas of the shirts had come to his mind. He seemed a bit sheepish about having contradicted the association that he himself had made. He acknowledged that it must represent part of the trend we had discussed in the previous session, of wishing to be in his father's place and have his father's authority.

In this minute segment of an analysis, we can perceive the manifold ramifications of the patient's conflicts. Let us examine only one set of phenomena pertaining to the conflict over the wish to acquire his father's prized possessions. When derivatives of this impulse begin to attain the quality of consciousness, the patient's response is an immediate denial followed by an affirmation. He does not know where the watch is—yes, he does, his brother has it. He never wanted it—yes, he did, not for himself but for his daughter. He did not get the watch, but in the dream it ends up in his possession. However, he cannot put it into his pocket. In the dream, however, he is wearing his father's clothes. In reality, he cannot wear them nor can he get rid of them. The all-pervasive conflict is clearly manifest in the dream, in his associations and in his inhibition about wearing his father's clothes. His conscious concern about the brother's health is counterposed by a fantasy of inheriting the watch through his brother's death. The wish to steal is balanced off by the fear of being stolen from. The contributions of each one of the psychic agencies—ego, id, or superego—is apparent in the material, and the forms and methods of their combinations and compromise lay down distinct guidelines for the future course of therapy.

To return to the clinical material. Further attempts to probe the dream proved unsuccessful. He could make no associations to putting the watch in his pocket. He protested only that he was unable to do so, and that in the end the watch seemed to be in the process of being taken away from him. In an attempt to bring the dream and the material back into the context of the transference, I pointed out that this was a striking dream to have just before the vacation. The patient seemed surprised and said, "Is that right? I wonder why you think so." Then after a pause he said, "I'm supposed to come back on the Tuesday after Labor Day, but I won't be able to do it. I won't be back until the following Thursday."

So, on the next to the last working day before the vacation, the patient brought in a dream about the imminent departure of one of his employees and the threatened departure of his brother. His employee left her psychiatrist with his money in her possession, and in the dream the patient was left with his brother's, formerly his father's watch in his possession, after the brother's apparent demise. To oppose his acquisitive and hostile wishes, the patient enlisted a wide array of defensive maneuvers—reaction formation, denial, projection, displacement, and repression. The behavior of the patient toward the watch in the dream is duplicated exactly in his behavior toward the items of apparel that he had inherited from his father. He could not enjoy their use nor could he give them up. (Parenthetically, as a general rule in a dream, the behavior of the person depicted as the dreamer reflects the ego's attitude concerning the intrapsychic conflict. It is the attitude with which the dreamer readily identifies himself and which is most acceptable to him.) Inhibition, renunciation, and self-punishment are all apparent in this material. To repeat, the dynamic interplay of forces representative of ego, id, or superego functioning explicates the material most effectively and serves as a guide to the technical approach to the material.

The next, very brief example will illustrate how analyzing the clinical data within the framework of the structural hypothesis may afford precise criteria for the making of a very specific interpretation. This material is taken from the analysis of a patient being treated through a clinic. He is a brilliant man who had the misfortune of being born with a physical deformity that is clearly visible. Understandably, he is deeply enraged at his cruel fate.

At the beginning of the session, the patient began to elaborate, half in jest, half in earnest, various plans to put the leaders of the world in an embarrassing situation. Progressively the aggressive component of his fantasy became more open and clearer, eventuating in the thought of unleashing an atom bomb on the city of New York. After describing this fantasy with some relish, the patient added jocularly, "But of course I would give you some warning so you could get out of town." After a momentary pause, he asked the analyst, "Say, what about the confidentiality of the material that goes on here?"

The analyst responded with a question, "Why do you ask?" The patient's response was logical and precise. He said, "I have worked in clinics and I know the routines. Files are kept very loosely. Many people have access to the files. In your clinic I know that the patients are not identified by name but by number. However, with my defect, I would be readily recognizable by anybody who reads the chart or to the secretaries who do the typing." The analyst did not respond to this statement, and the patient continued with his associations, the significance of which do not concern us at this present time.

The reality of the patient's concern is not the issue here. He could have posed the same question the first day he entered treatment and any time thereafter. The true significance of the question is established by its context in the material and its contiguity to a very specific thought, a thought that appeared in consciousness in the spirit of spoofing, and was cloaked in reaction formation. The thought concerned the wish to destroy not only the city of New York but the analyst as well. What was the nature of the patient's conflict at this moment? In part, he was opposed to his own hostility toward the analyst; it made him feel ashamed and guilty. Part of the inner dialogue had been omitted. The full text, if we could restore it, might have read something along these lines: "I'd like to kill everyone in the city, even my analyst. But that's not right. He's trying to help. It's a terrible thought. I'm ashamed of it. I don't like myself for thinking such thoughts. What would people think if they found out? I hope they never do." The contribution of each of the component parts of the psychic apparatus—ego, id, or superego—is clear enough and does not have to be elaborated.

Referring to the concern about confidentiality of the records, a more appropriate response on the part of the analyst might have been, "Why do you think this thought came to you just now?" The reality of the patient's concern is unquestionable, but the immediate significance of the concern is established by its context in the session and its contiguity to the specific reference to the analyst. The aggressiveness of the id and jocular defense of the ego are easy enough to discern, but the contribution of the superego can be clearly inferred by an examination of the dynamically determined sequence of elements in the patient's associations. Such an occasion could be an opportunity to open the exploration and discussion of the patient's guilt and of his need and concern for other individuals, elements in his psychology until now overshadowed by his bitterness against fate.

SUMMARY

In the opinion of this author, as far as clinical work is concerned, the structural hypothesis seems to be the most useful and effective set of concepts to apply to the data of observation obtained within the psychoanalytic situation. More than any other model of the mind, it clarifies the vicissitudes of intrapsychic conflict and accordingly helps establish criteria for the validation of interpretations and reconstructions, as well as guidelines for the future course of therapy.

Chapter 3

The Klein–Bion Model

Hanna Segal, M.D.

In my view, the Klein–Bion model that I am using combines the structural model discussed in the previous chapter with the interpersonal model discussed in the next chapter.

The model of the mind developed by Melanie Klein in terms of the paranoid–schizoid and the depressive positions is a development of Freud's structural model. When Klein began working in the 1920s she used Freud's structural model as the basis of her work. Her investigations of the origins of the superego and its detailed composition led to her later formulations. She investigated the growth of both the ego and the superego and the relationship between them in terms of the development of object relationships, external and internal. The study of early introjective and projective processes threw light on the structure of the ego as well as the superego—for instance, the enrichment of the ego by introjections and its impoverishment by projection into the superego.

The danger in presenting any model is that it is schematic—a skeleton without flesh. In presenting a model one cannot convey the infinite variety of human relationships and emotions. It also seems repetitive: for instance, in his last book Lebovici says Kleinian analysis is so repetitive, always dealing with the shift between the paranoid–schizoid and the depressive positions. In the same way one could say that the Oedipus complex is repetitive, since we are always concerned with it, and yet we know that it contains all the infinite richness of human experience.

In the Kleinian model, the human psyche has two basic positions. By position Klein means a particular constellation of basic object relationships, external and internal, fantasies, anxieties, and defenses. Though they arise out of developmental stages, she does not call them stages, since they determine basic structures which persist throughout life. The paranoid–schizoid position is the earlier one; the later, depressive position leads to maturity. But that maturity is never complete and there are always fluctuations between the two positions—the predominance of the depressive promoting development and maturity, and the predominance of the paranoid–schizoid creating a disturbance in development, which may culminate in illness.

The paranoid–schizoid position is the infant's earliest relationship to the world. Emerging from the chaotic welter of internal and external perceptions at birth, the infant tries to organize his perceptions and instinctual drives and emotions by means of splitting. In this splitting he attributes all love, goodness, and bliss to an ideal object and all distress to a bad object. A hungry infant does not have the capacity to experience the absence of a good feeding breast; what he experiences is being gnawed by hunger like a bad internal breast. The absence of satisfaction is felt as a persecution by a bad object. All love and desire is directed to the ideal object which the infant wants to introject, possess, and identify with. All hatred is both directed to the persecutory object and projected onto it, since the infant wants to rid himself of everything within that is felt to be bad and disruptive. What Freud calls the death instinct, which threatens the infant from within, is partly projected onto the bad object and partly converted into aggression against it. The leading anxiety is paranoid and hypochondriacal; the leading mechanisms of defense are splitting, as described, projection, and projective identification and idealization.

The concept of projective identification is important to an understanding of the Kleinian model of the mind. In projective identification not only impulses but parts of the ego are projected onto the object. Thus, the superego not only contains the projected id impulses, as in Freud's model, it contains projected parts of the ego itself. In fact, we doubt whether there ever is a pure projection of impulse without a projective identification of the part of the ego relating to that impulse. Thus, the early superego would be experienced in a very bodily fashion. Through a projection in fantasy of the infant's own bodily organs, qualities and perceptions belonging to the ego can equally be projected into the superego. H. Rosenfeld describes an acute schizophrenic who had three superegos—brown cow, yellow cow, and wolf, corresponding to his oral, urinary, and fecal impulses respectively (Rosenfeld, 1952).

Excessive anxiety leads also to fragmentation, giving rise to typical schizoid fears of annihilation and disintegration. Another feature of excessive anxiety is what Bion described as pathological projective identification (Bion, 1957). In pathological projective identification part of the ego is fragmented and projected onto the object, fragmenting it, and giving rise to terrifying perceptions of what he calls "bizarre objects"—those objects being fragments of the object, containing projected fragments of the self and imbued with hostility and anxiety. For instance, a patient of mine experienced an approaching psychotic episode as his mind being invaded by millions of little computers which would destroy it. In fact, on that occasion the episode was contained in the analysis and he did not break out into a psychosis, as had happened previously. We understood first that the millions of computers were all my interpretations over the years having become concrete persecutory objects in his mind. But we also understood the origin of this perception. The patient had occasion to use a computer in his work. He lived in grandiose computer fantasies for weeks. He had a fantasy that he would get access to an endless supply of small pocket computers and supply all departments of British universities with them and by means of those computers dominate the whole of British university life. Underlying that was an unconscious fantasy that by means of his computers he would defeat me and all psychoanalysis. The little computers represented both his semen and babies and fragments of his own personality invading the world. The projection of those fragments, meant to dominate and disintegrate me, changed me into a collection of little computers invading him back. Every interpretation became a bizarre object in his mind. The understanding of that situation enabled him to return, at least for the time being, to a more normal perception of me as a person to whom he felt hostile and whom he wanted to dominate, and it freed him from threatening hallucinations and delusions.

In favorable circumstances in the infant's early life the good experiences predominate over the bad ones. This strengthens his belief in the existence of a good object and in his own capacity to love. The introjection of the ideal object forms the root of the ego ideal aspect of the superego, but insofar as the infant also identifies with this internal object, it strengthens the ego and promotes its growth. When this happens, the stronger ego of the infant is less driven to project its hatred, and therefore, the bad experiences are less colored by violent projections of hatred, and the power of bad objects diminishes. In those circumstances a gradual integration occurs and the infant approaches the depressive position. The depressive position is defined by Klein as the infant's relation to the mother as a whole object. The infant begins to realize that his good and bad experiences come from the same object and from himself as the same infant who can both love and hate his parent. I say parent because, with the discovery of whole people and their interrelationships, the depressive position initiates early forms of the Oedipal complex. With the discovery of this ambivalence and the growing capacity to recognize absence and loss, the infant or growing child is open to feelings of guilt over hostility to a loved object and loss and mourning. The working through of this situation of mourning initiates reparative feelings and capacities for symbolization and sublimation, and reinforces loving and reparative drives and concerns in the genital position. The capacity of the child to cope with the depressive position in a growth-promoting way depends partly on external circumstances. In unfavorable circumstances the excessive pain promotes the deployment of manic defenses or a regression to paranoid–schizoid ones. But it also depends on the previous stage: If the bad self and object are felt to be much stronger than the ideal one, integration is felt as the destruction of the little good one possesses. If fragmentation predominates, integration is not possible, since bizarre objects can only be conglomerated. You cannot integrate a good mother out of a million little computers.

At this point I will present my model schematically: In the object relationship in the paranoid–schizoid position, the relation is to a part object, also split into an ideal persecutory one. The ego is similarly split. In the depressive position, the relation is to integrated parents, loved and hated. The ego is more integrated. The paranoid–schizoid superego is split between an excessively idealized ego ideal and an extremely persecutory superego. In the depressive position, it is a hurt loved object with human features.

The change is of course gradual, and in the transition, most frequent in the neurotic, is a superego which contains both paranoid and depressive features, giving rise to persecutory guilt. The leading anxiety in the first position is of persecution, fragmentation, or annihilation. In the second position, the fear is of guilt and the loss of a loved object. The reality sense in the first position is grossly distorted by projections. As projections diminish in the depressive position, the reality sense gains ascendence; the reality sense both about the nature of the external world, and the inner psychic reality; that is, the nature of one's own impulses and fantasies. In this way omnipotence is gradually diminished. Thus, a move from one position to the other is a move from predominantly psychotic to nonpsychotic functioning.

Thus, like Freud's structural model the structure of the personality is seen as a function of the relationship between the ego and the internal object which is also built partly on perception and partly on projection. The difference is that in the Kleinian model the structure is one evolved out of a variety of internal objects and it changes in character as the child develops. The projections into this internal figure are not only of impulses, but of parts of the ego. The ego itself is affected by projective and introjective processes. In Freud's model the superego is an object introjected at the end of the Oedipal phase. In Klein's model, it is a structure evolved from infancy onwards.

I said that this model is both structural and interpersonal. It is interpersonal in that it relates the development of the ego and the internal objects to personal relationships, since at every stage the infant's fantasies are modified by the actual experience of his interaction with the environment. Bion in particular made a study of the effects of mother's response to the early infantile projections and the way it affects the whole growth of the mental apparatus.

The interpersonal nature of the process is most evident in the consulting room. Core fantasies which became structuralized are mobilized again in the transference, and what became purely intrapsychic becomes again interpersonal. The patient projects his internal objects into the analyst. The analyst is not only an object of his impulses, but the patient tries to use him as a part of his defensive structure, as he used his objects in the past; and the analyst's response is as crucial as was the response of his environment in the formative years. There is a constant pressure on the analyst to act out his appointed role in the patient's defensive system. This pressure and the analyst's own response to it has to be recognized and acknowledged. The analyst's own pathology will frequently impinge on the process, and that and its effect on the patient has to be carefully monitored.

We must always watch the interplay of the transference and countertransference and be aware of our own contribution and the way it affects the patient, as the infantile part of the patient will react to our reality in much the same way it reacted to his real objects in infancy.

I do not propose to go here into the details of technique. This may be best left to the discussion. But to keep to the theme, I would like to give an example of how I understand the clinical material in terms of the models of the mind. I put the word *models* in the plural because I am aware that I may use slightly varying models according to the situation. For instance, in situations when there is a problem of communication or acting on, I am more likely to think in terms of a Bion model of container and contained (mother's response to the infant's projective identifications and its effects on the mental apparatus ([Bion, 1962].) In other situations I may keep more in mind other aspects of the model, like a precise shift between persecutory and depressive feelings. I should like to add here that I, of course, do not consciously use the model in listening to the patient, but just try to understand what he communicates to me. Nevertheless, I am aware that models exist in my preconscious or unconscious, and inevitably provide me with a framework which makes the material more understandable. I wish to describe what I consider to be a shift in the patient's structure as seen in terms of the framework.

Mr. A. came into analysis in his early thirties. He was not working anywhere near his true potential; his sexual life was a mess, dominated by pornographic fantasies and masturbation, with a few very unsatisfactory sexual relationships with women. He was given to severe attacks of panic related, it soon appeared, to underlying megalomanic fantasies. I would not describe him as a borderline, but rather as a severe neurotic. He did, however, suffer also from occasional, and when very anxious, frequent, hallucinatory episodes. These were not truly psychotic hallucinations, since he was aware they were hallucinations, and with a tremendous effort, could always struggle out of them. Over the years we understood that those hallucinatory episodes were linked with violent projective fantasies of a very invasive kind. In childhood and young adulthood they were associated with anal masturbation, and later, with equivalents of anal masturbation. The projected parts of himself would get identified with part of his object, which led to concretization. And those parts would then invade him, much as I described in the other patient with the little computers. For instance, he had a hallucination of a motorcyclist riding into his head. But the motorcyclist's head also looked like a finger. The underlying fantasy was that as he masturbated with his finger in his anus, he was in fact penetrating my anus and the finger-motorcyclist became a part of me that would invade him. You will notice that the degree of fragmentation is much less than in the more psychotic patient who had a million little computers in his head. In this patient, too, there were more fragmented perceptions, but a part of his ego was always unfragmented and kept its perceptions—he knew he was hallucinating.

I will now report a dream, after which, the hallucinations disappeared completely and permanently.

One day he told me that, as he was going past my consulting room door to the waiting room, he became very anxious because the thought occurred to him that there was no guard at the door and nothing to stop him from getting into the consulting room and interfering with the session of my other patient. Then he added, "Come to think of it, there is nothing to stop me doing what I want on the couch. For instance, if I wanted to, I could lie upside down." Then he giggled, and became embarrassed as he realized that upside down in the bed is the position he was in during some loveplay with his girl friend the night before. So, apparently the situation was as follows: There is no guard at the door, no husband. He could have intercourse with me as his girl friend and have our positions upside down; that is, with him dominating me—apparently, a plain Oedipal situation. He went on to tell me a dream. He said: "I had a dream in which I was explaining to M. (the girl friend) about my hallucinations. I was telling her, 'Look, I dream up a car and there it is.' And the car appeared." He got into the front seat. But there was no partition between front and back—no pole to lean against. He started falling backwards, feeling an utmost panic. And he woke up with severe anxiety.

My understanding of his associations preceding the telling of the dream, and the dream was as follows:

The pole is a phallic symbol. But also, I am of Polish origin, and my husband's name is Paul. In the absence of the pole, the father, or the penis in the vagina, there is nothing to stop him not just from having intercourse with his mother on a genital level, there is nothing to stop him from restrained projective identification with her, leading to the loss of boundaries, confusion, and panic. In this dream the father's penis is absent, but in other dreams or hallucinations, the persecutory penis would return, as in the hallucinations of the motorcyclist.

Two years later, having changed very considerably, he was getting married. A few days before the wedding his relationship to me, mostly in paternal transference, was rather ambivalent. He was very grateful to me, but also experienced me as an obstacle. He thought I would be angry at his taking a few days off from his analysis for his honeymoon. He also split between me and his real father. His father would have wanted him to be married in church. I would be angry at such hypocrisy. When he came back from his honeymoon he said that he had never been so moved in his life as he was at the actual wedding ceremony. He did marry in church. As they sang the hymn, "The Lord Is My Shepherd," which was his dead father's favorite hymn, he was overwhelmed with emotion. He had never been so happy and so unhappy at one and the same time. He didn't know if at the moment he was regaining his father or losing him. He was so aware of his father's presence in his thoughts, and so acutely aware of his real absence at the wedding. He then told me a dream he had the night before the wedding.

He dreamed that a fisherman promised to teach him fishing. The fisherman arrived, but his hands were very cut and bandaged. Mr. A. thought that he wouldn't be able to come out fishing. But the fisherman said, no, he was all right and he would take him and teach him fishing all the same.

His first association was that on the last day before he left for his wedding, I drew his attention to the fact that his remarks to me were very cutting.

Putting it schematically, in the first dream reported, the relation is to a part object—the penis/the pole. The mother, represented by the car is a cloaca—no partition between front and back. One could say also that front and back have no human features. His relationship to his object, the car, is one of violent projective identification, leading to fragmentation and disintegration. The result is depersonalization, acute anxiety, and confusion. In this case the experience has been expressed and contained in a dream, evidence, I think, of working through and integrating.

In the second dream his relation is to whole objects. The father exists as a person to whom he is related in an ambivalent way and whom he can introject as a helpful figure—the internal potent father whom he needs in his internal world in order to be able to marry. Such an introjection contributes to his masculine identity and potency. In the church he experiences a mourning for his father which he had never really felt before, admitting the pain of the real loss, but also the happiness of having regained an inner perception of his father of a kind he was never previously aware of.

In this session the change is evident mostly in relation to the father. But there was a similar change in his relation to the maternal figure, resulting in what proved in years to come to be an extremely happy and stable marriage.

I would see this material as a gradual but basic shift from a predominantly paranoid–schizoid position with a prevalence of projective identification and fragmentation, to the depressive position, with an introjection of ambivalently loved objects, in which ambivalent love predominates over hatred. Omnipotence is also diminished; thus, the wounds inflicted by his cutting remarks are not irreparable, and the analyst–father can continue to function in a helpful way. And speaking of the plurality of models, I suppose that at that point the predominant model in my mind would be Freud's genital Oedipus complex with castration anxiety. But in the back of my mind, I would have had a model consisting of all the shifts in the patient's structure and in our relationship, for him to experience his Oedipus complex in a way so different from that of two years earlier.

His troubles, of course, are by no means completely over. His omnipotent fantasies are still around and interfere with his functioning. And he still resorts to projective identifications, which weaken his ego. Nevertheless, some basic stability has been achieved at a depressive level, projective identifications are more coherent, less omnipotent, do not turn into hallucinations, and are more easily reintegrated. He is not at risk of breaking down or being subject to crippling panics.

I will now elaborate on two basic points: First, I will elaborate on why frustration is experienced as persecution in the paranoid–schizoid position.

To experience frustration one has to have the memory of a good object and good experience, as well as the concept of time and absence. Those concepts are not yet available to the very young infant. There is satisfaction or pain; what is *is*, one is attacked by something bad. The language reflects it: one is "gnawed by hunger," "the wolf is at the door." In French slang to be hungry is to feed on a mad cow, "manger de la vache enragée." So hunger gnaws, devours one like a wolf or a mad breast (cow).

Furthermore, because of constant projections there is always a bad object around. In his essay "Negation" (Freud, 1925b), Freud says the infant's first relation to the world is "that I'll take in—that I'll spit out." Everything felt as bad—experience, object, the infant's own impulses—is projected out onto the breast making it a bad object full of the frustrated infant's own impulses (the wolf—the mad cow). The advent of hunger or pain is then attributed to that object.

I will now discuss further Bion's model of mental functioning in terms of "container and contained" and the mother as container of "projective identifications." Bion extends Klein's work on early projective identifications. The infant in fantasy projects onto the breast unintegrated, misunderstood painful experiences—pain, fear of death, or hatred often identified with concrete substances, like wind, urine, feces. But it is not in fantasy only because the mother is affected by the infant's state of mind. For Bion those early projective identifications are a first method of communication. The baby "screams out" his painful state and the mother experiences anxiety and pain and responds. A mother who can contain the infant's distress without rejecting it or collapsing herself makes the right response—feeding, burping, changing diapers, or providing just the right emotional response for comfort.

Thus the infant gets back not the projected "bad," but something good, which makes sense of his experience. And the infant introjects not only his own experience "detoxicated," but he also introjects the breast as a container capable of bearing anxiety and modifying it. This is a precondition for the elaboration of the depressive position.

This modification of projections through their being contained and modified by maternal care is responsible for the gradual lessening of persecution. (If mother cannot perform this function the infant's projections remain unaltered or become worse.)

Bion also evolved a theory of thinking based on the transformance of what he calls beta elements—crude, concrete, and primitive, into alpha elements, those of dream thought. The alpha function is first performed unconsciously by mother converting the received crude projections into thought, and is then introjected by the infant. It is beyond the scope of this chapter to attempt to elaborate further upon Bion's ideas.

Finally, I will comment briefly on the question of the relation of Klein's "depressive position" to Mahler's "individuation and separation." I believe the depressive position was described a good while before Mahler. And I'm not aware, though I may have missed them, of any of Mahler's writings correlating her concept to the existing one of the depressive position.

Certainly, there is a major difference in Klein's and Mahler's views of the preceding stage. Mahler's idea of "fusion" before separation and individuation is certainly very different from Klein's idea of the paranoid–schizoid position. We would view fusion as a result of projective identification into an ideal object and if it amounts to more than transitory states we would view it as a defense against anxiety of a paranoid nature.

Chapter 4

The Interpersonal (Sullivanian) Model

Edgar Levenson, M.D.

The French poet, Paul Valéry (1956), said that the artist of modern sensibility must spend his time trying to see what is visible, and, more important, trying *not* to see what is invisible. Philosophers, he said (and he might well have added, psychoanalysts) pay a high price for striving to achieve the opposite. To the extent that one can encompass an entire psychoanalytic posture within a brief presentation, this might be said to be the essence of interpersonal psychoanalysis. The data of psychoanalysis is, first and foremost, what can be *observed:* the patient in his reported interactions with others, past and present; and the patient's interactions with the therapist as they can be directly observed in the therapy relationship. Dreams, fantasies, free associations, slips are in no sense disregarded, but they are seen as efforts the patient is making, through imagery and imagination, to grapple with and comprehend experience. However distorted or caricatured it might appear to be, fantasy is considered more the reflection of poorly comprehended real-life interpersonal experience than the emergence from the depths of solipsistic, primitive impulses.

Sullivan (1956) said that "no one has grave difficulties in living if he has a very good grasp of what is happening to him." He felt that vital interactions between the patient and significant other people were "selectively inattended"; that is, scrupulously *not* noticed. Why? He postulated that this was due to anxiety—not what we ordinarily mean by anxiety, but a feeling more akin to dread, terror, and so disruptive to both the patient and the necessary people in his life that, to avoid its contagion, they do not see what is there to be seen. It is not fear of the loss of the helper, as Bowlby (1973) would have it, but fear of fear itself.

This anxiety about anxiety is central to understanding the difference between Freud's and Sullivan's position. Sullivan felt that there was, from inception, an empathic bond between the mother and child. If the mothering person became anxious, the child was flooded with an overwhelming, calamitous panic. One notes that this anxiety is communicated interpersonally. The extreme reaction of the child may well be inappropriate to the degree of the stimulus, because the child's defenses against this flooding have not been yet adequately developed.

These defenses against anxiety constitute what Sullivan called the "self-system." This is not the *self* in its usual sense of the total unique personality of the person; but rather a series of strategies for coping with anxiety, "security operations," which become more elaborate and sophisticated as the child ages. Again, one must be clear that these defenses do not operate, as in the Freudian system, against unconscious internal drives but against a contagious terror set in motion *by the other person.* These defenses are elaborated into internalized percepts, very similar to the object relations self-objects. The child decides that what elicits anxiety in the parenting person is the "Bad Me"; what propitiates them is the "Good Me." A unique contribution developing from Sullivan's pioneering work with schizophrenics was his concept of "Not Me"—those interpersonal transactions which call out really extreme anxiety from the parenting person, and so disorganize the child that he experiences the exchange as "uncanny" and depersonalizes it. This experience of the uncanny is so catastrophic that it can precipitate a psychotic experience.

In a small way, most of us have experienced this feeling in those nightmares which wake us up in a terror and where the feeling of eeriness hangs on throughout the waking day. Sullivan (1953, p. 191) has an excellent report of his own experience with such a dream.

This rather primitive self-concept of "Good Me," "Bad Me," and "Not Me" is later elaborated into a complex mélange of avoidances, inattentions, interpersonal strategies, and tactical misrepresentations. For example, a child of a schizophrenic mother who is made acutely anxious by the child's needs for intimacy and closeness, learns to deny the need for closeness, to not see it when it is offered, to misdirect the offering other, and to either drive away or convert to coldness anyone potentially proffering closeness. To do so entails a large number of fantasies and distortions about oneself and others, but these distortions are in the service of interpersonal security. Distortion is not a residue of instinctual forces, but of interpersonal events.

The concept of the unconscious in Sullivan is somewhat elusive, since there is some implication that the patient knows what he is not supposed to know he knows—an idea that Sartre (1953) and R. D. Laing (1967) later developed at length. Why Sullivan leaned so heavily on anxiety is too complex an issue for this short exegesis; I think that he might have as easily assumed that inattention resulted from obfuscated or confused messages from others (see Levenson [1983] for elaboration of this issue).

Sullivan's original position was an amalgam of Adolph Meyer's meticulously data-oriented institutional psychiatry with two prevalent American philosophical movements, *pragmatism* and *operationalism*. The pragmatism of Dewey, James, and Peirce claimed that all concepts can only be derived from sensory data. Bridgeman's operationalism stated that you can't observe something without in some way becoming part of what you set out to observe and changing both it and you, and the very observation, by virtue of your participation. To put it simply: What you see is what you get and you are part of it! It is a little like that famous comic-strip possum, Pogo's, classic aphorism, "We have met the enemy and they is us!"

This amalgam was further peppered with borrowings from the Chicago School of Sociology, from Sapir, Mead, and Benedict in anthropology, from linguistics, and even from Korzybski's general semantics. Language, and the social and personal use of language (what the semioticists call the "pragmatics" of language) were of great interest to Sullivan. He saw language not simply as a commentary on experience but as the primary mode for the conceptualization of experience. Language was the instrument par excellence of the self-system; not fantasy and not imagery. Sullivan very much presaged later psychoanalytic interest in semiotics and hermeneutics. As Crowley (1984) put it, "Sullivan clearly saw unconscious thoughts and feelings as unformulated experience to be remedied by the analytic process of putting what is unformulated into words understandable by another person" (p. 177).

Sullivan, a self-confessed autodidact, incorporated virtually every aspect of the social science explosion of the 1940s. Sitting smack in the midst of these riches, he wove them into an interpersonal theory of psychiatry. You will note that Sullivan referred to his position as interpersonal *psychiatry*, not psychoanalysis. Although Sullivan was, very early, interested in Freud's novel theories, and did indeed write about them, the development of an interpersonal *psychoanalysis* was a somewhat later development, a synthesis of Sullivan's apple-pie American psychiatry and the European psychoanalysis which entered this country as a consequence of the Nazi-inspired diaspora. Along with Billy Wilder, Bertolt Brecht, and Albert Einstein came virtually the entire corpus of European analysts outside of Britain, including some, like Karen Horney, who were not Jewish but could not function in the Third Reich.

If, for the interpersonalists, what you see is what you get, for the Freudians, things are never what they seem. Coming from a traditional platonic position, the Europeans were interested in the reality *behind* the appearances. The surface was seen as a mask, hiding a deeper core of truth. When Horney and Fromm, Europeans to the bone, collated their position with that of Sullivan, a heady, near-indigestible brew resulted. It is hard to know, in the 1980s, precisely what Sullivan had in mind in 1940. We are reading him now through the filters of our own experience, not just with other theoretical formulations, but with a changing culture and its expectations. We are necessarily children of our own times. But this is an inevitable problem in interpretation or, more precisely, hermeneutics.

At any rate, this amalgam of two cultural streams was so powerful and dislocating that there remains a very wide variety of positions held under the loose rubric of "interpersonal." A strict concordance of views is no more possible with our group than with any other. Interpersonalists range from extreme interactionalists through viewpoints largely indistinguishable from object-relations theorists, especially Winnicott and Fairbairn, and even on to some closet 1930s Freudians. (Greenberg and Mitchell [1983] provide an excellent exegesis of Sullivan's location on the object-relations spectrum.) What I am presenting is, of course, a personal perspective and hardly an ex cathedra position. I am attempting to convey a posture about therapy, rather than a detailed blueprint of interpersonalism.

One must be very careful to respect the integrity of these differences. There is an automatic translation that occurs when one is presented with a different perspective, particularly if it emerges, as Kuhn (1962) put it, from a different paradigmatic stance. Sullivan's *selective inattention* is not "nothing but" Freud's *dissociation. Security operations* are not *defenses:* to blur these distinctions is to indulge in a false ecumenism. We are not talking about the same things using different words; we are using different words to delineate different perspectives on experience and on therapy.

That caveat notwithstanding, I would claim that the clear line of schism between interpersonalist and Freudian (increasingly also a loose coalition of positions) remains *the search for the truth behind appearances* versus *the search for the truth inherent in appearances.* For the Freudian, the key question is, what does it truly mean? For the interpersonalist, the question is, what's going on around here?

The idea that there is a deeper reality, that appearances are distortions, requires some version of a drive theory; that is, a powerful, unresolvable impulse or "instinct" which emerges from the depths, is defended against, and surfaces in a distorted form. Instinct *cannot* be neutralized by experience. Object-relations theory shifts the drive from libido to "object seeking," but predicates so early a conflict that the infant's primitive and phantasmagorical perceptions persist into later life. What Sullivan called "needs" rather than instincts, however, consist of an extending developmental matrix of interpersonal activity. Needs require the presence of another person. Needs may or may not be met, but if met they will abate. It can be seen that drives require *defenses:* needs require living *skills,* techniques for obtaining satisfactions from others, a cradle-to-grave process. I must reemphasize that, for Sullivan, the problem resides in the anxiety the needs provoke in the helping of other person, not in the inherent force of the need. Needs *need* not cause anxiety; it is not inherent in them. When they do, it is essentially an interpersonal process.

Sullivan (1953, p. 33) did have a theory of psychosocial development, but unlike Freud's epigenetic theory, it was based on the development of implementational skills in a social context, rather than on changing body zones. Moreover, it was not limited to infancy and early childhood, but emphasized particularly the developmental epochs leading to adulthood. Briefly, Sullivan's schema started with *infancy* which extended until the development of speech, whether that speech has meaning or not. *Childhood*, next, which extended to the appearance of the need for playmates. The *juvenile era* extended through the elementary school years to the need for an intimate relationship with another person of "comparable status." The *preadolescent period*, of great importance to Sullivan, ends with the eruption of puberty and its consequent genital sexuality and psychology with the shift of interest from a person of one's own sex to a heterosexual object. *Adolescence* is the period in which sexual and social relations are solidified. *Late adolescence* is when the patterns of socialization are fully established. And finally, *adulthood,* the culminating period in which love for another is established; that is, not simply genital lust or need for closeness, but a fully elaborated caring and respect for another person. (See Chatelaine [1981, pp. 45–46] for a detailed presentation of Sullivan's "heuristic" stages.)

One notes that, for Sullivan, emphasis is as much on the period when restitution is possible, as on the period in which the damage occurs. Although schizophrenic destiny begins with a disruption of the earliest infantile empathy, for Sullivan, preadolescence was considered the period wherein potential schizophrenics often failed to achieve intimacy with a friend and fell by the wayside. Note that whatever the failures of the past, the person has a current opportunity to develop a competence which will carry him through a precarious period. As Sullivan (1956) said, "I am much more interested in what can be done than in what has happened" (p. 195). The thrust of treatment is to learn a far more flexible and sensitive way of perceiving and engaging one's interpersonal world. It follows then that the transference–countertransference is seen, not so much as a relatively pristine area in which to examine distortion carried over from the past, as it is a highly visible, present field for correlating what has happened in the past and what happens now between the patient and other people—*in this case,* the therapist, presumably an expert in relationships. Sullivan felt that when the patient, as known to himself, is the same as the patient as known to other people, one has achieved a psychiatric cure. Social cure requires a further development of social skills, leading to a more abundant life in the community.

This polarization of positions, albeit schematized and oversimplified, remains entirely relevant. Even though analytic institutes have, mercifully, largely divested themselves of their monolithic postures, I believe that this basic paradigmatic schism still permeates clinical material and if analysts lined up according to how they apply these distinctions to their clinical work, some very strange bedfellows indeed would emerge.

Yet, for all this apparent disarray in the ranks, fortunately there does remain a very powerful, jointly held core of psychoanalysis—something we can all agree on. It lies not in that can of worms, metapsychology, but in the *act* of psychoanalysis—what we all do when we do what we know how to do (see Levenson [1983, pp. 53–88] for an elaboration of the praxis of therapy).

I think we could agree that, regardless of institutional affiliations, we all establish a careful frame of theory. We all solicit data, look for resonances in this data as it emerges in different parameters of the patient's presentation, and then use *our* relationship with the patient in such a way as to reinforce and explicate these resonances, as we see them. The data may be conceived of as free association, fantasy, or a detailed inquiry into the events being reported, but in each case the procedure is the same. We follow the line of associations, we look for connections, for recurrences of pattern, and we differ from other psychotherapies in our use of the relationship with the therapist, as Freud said, as a "playground" for the material under discussion, rather than as a tool for effecting change.

The psychoanalytic praxis, then, is triadic: we establish a framework of great constancy, we solicit data, and we use our relationship with the patient to mirror the patient's life, rather than as an active instrument of change. We avoid "manipulating" the transference; that is, we do not try to heal the patient through the transference as do more directive, focused psychotherapies (see M. Gill [1982] for discussion of this issue).

I would claim yet another striking communality in psychoanalytic technique. The cabalists say that God's mystery dwells in the particular. The psychoanalytic method, too, delves down through the specific to arrive at the abstract. *For us, metapsychological truths emerge from a meticulous inquiry into the particular.* I believe that the single, most specific failure in psychoanalytic method, regardless of metapsychological considerations, is to move prematurely from the explicit data of the patient's life to a more abstract interpretation. For psychoanalysts, the issue should be to search for what is not known, what is out of awareness, unattended to, dissociated, or repressed. Psychoanalysis ought not to aspire to better explanations of what the patient already knows.

I would like to use a clinical example from Kohut (1984) to elaborate this absolutely critical issue:

> A colleague whom I had analyzed for a number of years told me, as he reflected on what he had achieved during the treatment, that it was "ironical" that while psychoanalytic scuttlebutt had it that self psychologists underplayed human aggression and hostility (supposedly by being too "nice" to their analysands), it was in the analysis with me and not in his training analysis with an analyst who repeatedly and insistently confronted him with the evidence of his hostility (especially in the transference) that he had for the first time experienced—deeply and fully—an intense wish to kill. And he told me, in retrospect, of an analytic session long ago (I believe it was about a year or two into his analysis) when he experienced this wish for the first time—at least for the first time with unmistakable intensity. It occurred in the aftermath of the analysis of a dream—not a "self-state dream" I should note, in view of another set of misapprehensions about self psychology that has come our way—on which we had been working for several sessions. The dream in question had taken place in a city block not far from my office. The patient observed a frail man walking along the block that led to a broad boulevard where a statue of a husky, muscular, proud warrior on horseback stood. As the patient watched the man walking along slowly, unsteadily, and weakly, he noticed that the man was not real but some kind of straw doll. Overcome with anger, the patient plunged a knife several times into the straw doll man. To his amazement—there was no evidence of guilt or horror about the deed in the dream—thick red blood flowed out between the straw (p. 138).

Kohut says that the analyst patient, in his prior training analysis, had had similar dreams and the analyst, after listening to his associations, interpreted Oedipal hostility and "encouraged the patient to contact those feelings in the transference." The patient could not contact a genuine wish to 'kill the therapist, only "moderate conscious anger" at the therapist for not being able to help him. One does hope that Kohut wondered if perhaps the patient was not making a "strawman" of his previous therapist. The interpreting seems banal, simply "the better explanation of what the patient already knows" that I referred to.

Kohut does something different in his interpretation: he focuses on the patient's real experience with his chronically ill father who died when he was eleven, and his transferential perception of an ill and enfeebled therapist. The interpretation was that "the patient was still trying to get to a strong father (the statue of the man on horseback) and that he was disappointed and frustrated because I was not such a father." Kohut implies, but does *not* make explicit, that the patient may have been reacting to real factors in his "transferential" response to the therapist as weak and ill.

The patient is able to come into touch with his rage at his father, what Kohut calls the "wish to get rid of the sick and depressed Father." Note that a repressed wish is still implicit. Kohut's interpretation, far richer than the first analyst's reductive formulation, utilizes both intrapsychic fantasy and real interpersonal experience previously ignored. It focuses the transference in a much more integrated way. The interpretation also permits the patient to "look at" the therapist, and to validate, without fear of destroying him, the possibility that the therapist may, too, be ill and lacking in "emotional vigor." Clearly, this formulation of Kohut's delves far deeper into the particulars of the patient's life; his universal fantasies, to be sure, but also the idiosyncratic life experiences which have shaped his defenses.

Yet, supposing one sinks further into the particulars, the

details. Dreams, I think, usually demonstrate a dialectic between this and that—two polarities of the same metaphor. Here it is lifelessness; the statue and the strawman are both effigies. One is, however, very powerful, perhaps dictatorial and to be admired or feared (the proverbial Man on Horseback). The other is feeble, slight, but equally unreal, a strawman. If the metaphor is lifelessness, the polarities are between the relative powers of the effigies, but also between bloodlessness and bloody. In rage, the patient plunges a knife into an effigy, a strawman (one set up to be easily defeated) and discovers to his amazement (but not horror) that the effigy bleeds. In a word, the patient is amazed to discover that the strawman is human, after all. Kohut makes no point at all of the patient's surprise at the blood. Rather, he focuses on the issue of rage.

What more likely effigy is there than the therapist, set up in the transference as either dictator or weakling, but in either case defined as a figment of the patient's fantasies? Could one perhaps postulate that the dream means exactly what it says, namely that the patient is amazed that the therapist is real, that he can be hurt, that he is vulnerable? Is it possible that the patient had in some previous session "gotten to" Kohut, hurt him? Could the patient's problem be, not his rage, but his sense of impotence, his inability to have *any* effect on a therapist who insists that he is not really seen by the patient, that what the patient thinks occurs is his fantasy projections?

The patient expects to rage at the strawman but does not expect to draw blood. What possible value can anger have, if it is directed against an unreal person? Real effect *always* must imply an authentic risk; to feel is to be endangered. Perhaps the effectiveness of Kohut's interpretation depended more on his admission of participation and vulnerability than on its correctness as doctrine.

What would have happened had Kohut asked the patient about his sense of the therapist's vulnerability? Perhaps the patient would have recalled a moment of panic in a previous session when he felt he had penetrated the therapist's neutrality.

Would this not be empathically communicated anxiety? Would not the self-system of the patient operate to "inattend" this event caused by the "Bad Me"? Kohut, by his strong and effective interpretation, shows the patient a paradoxical truth: the therapist is tacitly admitting weakness while being very forthright and strong as an analyst. The analyst bleeds—but not much! A subtle countertransference may be at play.

I have taken the particulars of the dream much further than either the first training analyst or Kohut. But it seems to me that this is the essence of Sullivan's concept of the detailed inquiry. As one engages and enriches the textural quality of the inquiry, it does not become more diffuse and confusing, but opens the door to transference. The very pursuit of specifics brings the therapist in, since one cannot inquire without selection or answer without recognizing the presence of the other person.

One could stop there: in Kohut's case it would have been established that the patient was concerned about the therapist's vulnerability; that is the patient's "fantasy." One might go further and ask whether there is some truth in the patient's perception and whether the recognition of that truth is necessary for the patient's cure.

In either case, the abstract formulations, the interpretations of content (of what the transactions are presumed to *really* mean) emerge quite effortlessly. For, as the Sufis say, "No problem is too difficult for a theoretician!" The interpretations may not come out the same for each therapist–patient dyad. After all, what the therapist saw in Kohut's patient's dream may depend, not only on his metapsychology, but to a considerable extent on his state of health. I suspect that the moment of countertransference for all therapists comes when they lift their noses from the text and begin to search about for encompassing formulations, attributions of meaning. The therapist's discipline lies in tolerating disorder.

Menninger and Holzman (1958) have made much the same point from a different theoretical perspective, when they say there is an automatic flow from the present reality situation into the analytic situation and then into the past. This "counterclockwork" progression is "the typical, proper and correct sequence" (p. 154). The function of the therapist is to facilitate this flow and then correlate it. It is here that the paths diverge, perhaps irrevocably. As I pointed out earlier, for the interpersonalist, this orderly sequence is not used to impress on the patient how the past is projected onto the present in the transference, but as an opportunity to show the patient how the same patterning of interpersonal experience, described and delineated on the "outside," is now actually occurring in the "inside"—the relationship of the patient and therapist. Hoffman (1983), in an excellent paper, locates psychoanalysts on a continuum defined by their use of the patient–therapist relationship as a piece of reality. As one might expect, interpersonalists seem to cluster rather to the left, although I must repeat my earlier caution that there is a wide range of diversity on this issue among interpersonalists. As M. Gill (1983) put it in his thoughtful examination of this issue, there are two major cleavages in psychoanalytic thought:

> One cleavage is between the interpersonal paradigm and the drive-discharge paradigm. The other cleavage is between those who believe the analyst inevitably participates in a major way in the analytic situation and those who don't. . . . I had assumed that these two cleavages ran parallel to each other, or at least those who adhered to the interpersonal paradigm would also ascribe to the analyst a major participation in the analytic situation.
>
> That I made this assumption implied an intrinsic connection between the interpersonal paradigm and a major participation on one hand, and the drive paradigm and a minor participation on the other. . . .
>
> I believe it can be demonstrated that there is no such intrinsic connection (p. 201).

To put it succinctly, analysts may be using the same methodology to obtain data, but then interpreting and applying it to different ends, either to lift distortion or to focus experience. At least in his view of therapist participation, Sullivan clearly would have been aligned with the former position, the alleviation of distortion. "Consensual validation" was intended to help the patient distinguish between what was real and appropriate and what was not. The present range of transference/ countertransference elaborations described by Epstein and Feiner (1979) cannot be attributed to Sullivan, who may well have pointed in that direction, but did not arrive there. Sullivan seems to have regarded transference and countertransference much as does Gill, as a variety of resistance, but unlike Gill (1983, p. 29), rather than analyze it, he preferred (as he did with dreams) to minimize it and get on with the work, the examination of real events in the patient's life.

I will use a second case vignette to limn out some of the implications inherent in a radical use of the patient–therapist relationship as a fertile field for interpersonal inquiry. Again, I must warn that this manner of working is not inevitable to the interpersonal position, but represents one of a number of possible permutations of the original Sullivanian thesis.

This patient is a man in his midthirties, attractive, charming, and at present successful. He has no neurotic symptoms, nor much apparent anxiety or depression. When he first came into therapy, he was suffering from a sense of alienation and indecision about his work and marital status. He was aware of a lack of intense feeling or commitment and distressed by his capacity for what Lifton called a protean response, that is, a capacity to fit in anywhere, be accepted anywhere, but never feel rooted in his own life. He is at present separated from his wife.

The present episode begins when this man, conscientious to a fault, does not appear for a session. For the first time in two years, he simply forgot. The next session he starts by announcing that he went to some trouble not to be late. He had to drop off his dirty laundry first with his housekeeper. He didn't want to bring it into the session with him. Twenty minutes later he says, "I really didn't want to tell you. I had sex over the weekend with this woman. . . . It was really very nice, pleasant . . . I'm not in love with her, though. [Long pause.] Funny thing, three days later, I got this prostatic pain. I thought, 'Sh-t, she gave me herpes!' " He checked with his physician who assured him it was nothing. That, of course, was the day he missed the session. Suddenly he recalls a childhood incident of being threatened by another boy on the street with a knife. He fended his assailant off by telling him that his father was a general in the army and would get him if any harm were done to his son. This took place overseas in an army of occupation post. His father was not a general. He doesn't know why, but he never told his parents of the incident.

Any analyst would hear the sequence, follow the thread of unconscious associations. He is clearly afraid to air his dirty laundry, his sexual success. He is afraid of retaliation from the therapist qua father. There is even, dare we say, the castrating knife. We have acting out, the violation of the frame of therapy (missing session, being late, withholding information). There is the flow of associations and the transference; he expects some retaliation from me, as the father, for his sexual prowess, which is perhaps even directed against me.

The patient is fascinated by the sequence when it is pointed out to him. He is delighted to see his Oedipus complex in operation. It is a case of, "By George! I really have an unconscious." He is also very quick to accept blame. He knows that his expectation of attack by the therapist is his "fantasy" based on distortions from the past. Was his father castrating? Only in fantasy. His father was, and is, in actuality, a very quiet, courteous man, never given to fits of rage or unreasonableness.

He is fifteen minutes late for the next session. One might reasonably suspect that he is trying to provoke a punitive response, to justify his fantasies of sexual triumph. Why was he late? He had spent the night with the very same woman, is coming to the session straight from her warm bed. He says,

"I had the crazy fantasy that you'd be jealous." Then, dutifully, he goes on to his fantasies of beating out father.

What the interpersonal therapist finds most relevant is, not this man's fantasies about parental retaliation, but the *way* he sets up the exchange; that he openly provokes a response and then acts as though it were not forthcoming. He has father nailed to the wall. This sly manner of provoking and then disowning the response is typical of him throughout all the parameters of his experience. As Hoffman (1983) put it, "The transference represents a way not only of construing but also of constructing or shaping interpersonal relations in general and the relationship with the analyst in particular" (p. 394).

The therapist has available a range of possible intercessions. Not responding clarifies nothing and provokes further acting out. The pattern of interaction may be pointed out to the patient dispassionately or the therapist may take a bolder leap, shift gears and say, "What makes you so sure that I'm not really jealous?" Patient (abashed): "What do you mean?" "Well, after all, you're an attractive young man, having all this fun. I'm a middle-aged therapist. Why wouldn't I be jealous?" The patient is devastated. How, then, can he count on the therapist's benevolence? Please note that the therapist has not confessed to envy; he has simply entertained the possibility.

It is inconceivable to me that this is a new idea to him. The possibility of the therapist's reaction is, after all, the essence of the entire exchange. What startles him really is that an interchange is called to his attention which in his past experience would have elicited so much anxiety that it would be selectively unattended to, not noticed by himself or other participants in the exchange. The therapist's query is, I repeat, not a confession, but an inquiry which shifts the issue from the patient's solipsistic fantasy to an *interaction* with the therapist, which is no less real because it proceeds by dialogue rather than action. One hopes to delineate with the patient the patterns of interaction which characterize his exchange with the therapist, and to clarify for him how these strategies of interaction (what Sullivan called the "self-system") were developed in his childhood as a way of coping with family experience.

In his family, *no one* admitted to evil thoughts, let alone contemplated evil deeds. It is a family of sins of omission. He was one of those unfortunate middle-class children who grow up in families where they are doomed never to be misunderstood. Oscar Wilde would have called this family decadent, which he defined as the wish to have feelings without paying the price. These parents do not admit to their own ambivalent feelings and do not engage the feelings of their children in any authentic way. To provoke ambivalent feelings in these parents is to provoke anxiety and to endanger the family security; not to evoke feelings is to succumb to alienation and detachment. The patient's past experience, his mode of dealing with it, and his recapitulation of it in the therapy is the heart of the matter. This is not to deny that there are pervasive, eternal father–son conflicts over sexuality and domination, but the universality of the conflict is less useful and interesting than the specific, unique patterns of coping which the patient has developed in his life.

Countertransference is no longer a contaminant of the field, but simply one pole of the transaction, the patient being the other. This viewpoint allows the therapist a wide spectrum of participations, but, I must emphasize, it does not encourage him to wild, "intuitive," corrective emotional experiences with the patient. The form of the participation is rigorously determined and contained by the material presented by the patient in the therapy. Grandiosity and self-indulgence on the part of the therapist are not encouraged.

Even in extreme versions of using the countertransference, one's experience is offered only as data, to be integrated with the patient's experience of the exchange. This data about the therapist's participation—the countertransference, if you will—*must* come out of the detailed inquiry. Otherwise, it becomes "empathic" or "intuitive" guessing which lends itself to further countertransferential obfuscation: it is not the Truth, indeed it well may be wrong. But as data it is relevant. (It is the countertransferential paradox: Can a therapist make a statement about his countertransference which is not countertransference?)

The therapist carefully avoids instrumental efforts; he is not trying to change anything. By widening the patient's awareness of his life, what Sullivan called an "expansion of the self" is arrived at. One then trusts that the patient can change his own life according to his own canons. Indeed, the therapist carefully avoids acting in a way he hopes will "cure" the patient. He is interested only in widening the circles of participant-observation for the patient, until a sufficient enrichment of his awareness of his life permits him to change.

The triad of containment, textual enrichment of data, and replay in the relationship with the therapist are held commonly by all analysts. The difference arises in the data focused. The interpersonalist does not so much look behind the data as at it. Hilda Bruch (1983), in describing her supervision with Sullivan, said that he advised her "to talk only about those things about which the patient or I could actually know something. I did exactly what he told me to do, and the patient was able to leave the hospital three months later" (p. 7).

In the process of extending the data of experience, the transference–countertransference is put to a somewhat different use, as an area of participant-observation of the patient's interactional patterns. It is still the search for what is not known and for how that knowledge is avoided, but in a different mode of inquiry. I suspect that, in doing what analysts do, we are all tapping into the same intrinsic process, a particular form of inquiry, but then using it to different ends. It would appear that these differences cut across the usual doctrinaire metapsychological groupings. Psychoanalysts may be redefining themselves and recoalescing around a novel set of issues. Rather than intrapsychic versus interpersonal or even, as Greenberg and Mitchell (1983) put it, drive–structure model versus relational–structural model; the core issue may well be the significance of distortion. Is transference a "playground" for elucidating and eliminating distortion; or is it a slice of life, intensified but yet made manageable by the constraints of the analytic frame? I believe that the interpersonal position is that people are made ill by their experience with other people, not by an inherent phantasmagoria. These distinctions may illuminate profoundly disparate positions on human relatedness and our helping role.

Chapter 5

Psychoanalytic Self Psychology

Arnold Goldberg, M.D.

INTRODUCTION

Since nature does not care how we choose to cut it up, to divide, and categorize it, we are free to devise our own forms; and this is true of physics as well as of psychology. The very idea of a discussion on models of the mind suggests that we can pick and choose among these models on some basis that goes beyond, or is parallel to, the question of what is the true, proper, and correct model. Is there a rational and factual way of assessing how the mind operates? Is there a practical way to choose the best model, or is it all a matter of personal comfort and choice? If nature does not care, then who can answer these questions?

Analysts of one persuasion or another usually see psychopathology as a series of developmental epochs, and they translate or interpret the patient's life to him according to their own world view or ideology or theory or even prejudice. Freud offered us a set of perspectives whereby we could understand what a patient was saying, by way of reenactment in the transference, at which point we could explain it to the patient by virtue of construction or reconstruction. Convinced as we may be of the truth or correctness of our theory or interpretations, we have all learned that therapists of different persuasions are similarly convinced and often similarly effective. That is one reason why it often seems an exercise in futility for analysts who employ different theories to listen to clinical material in order to determine who is "right." Any Kleinian can hear and see depressive and paranoid positions just as easily as Kohutians can spot selfobject failure, and classical analysts can perceive Oedipal vicissitudes. Either we retreat to isolated schools of beliefs, or else we are forced into some sort of relativism of analyst–patient narratives which have no basis in fact.

The last word is the problem: just what are the facts and what was the patient's life really like? This is the critical issue that compels many analysts to return to the posits of so-called natural science in order to gain a solid base of truth and fact. These familiar guidelines of positivism or neopositivism or empiricism state that we are able: (1) to gather objective data; (2) to construct logical hypothetico-deductive theories; (3) to develop laws that are not connected either to the objects of our study or to the investigator; (4) to put these facts into an exact and formal language; and (5) to test our theories by way of these self-subsistent facts. Supposedly this is the real home of science, exemplified by disciplines such as physics, and this will be the answer to the relativism or even the mysticism of the newly popular hermeneutics.

Many psychoanalysts insist that over time we will be able to formalize our theories. They are thus involved in the accumulation of data from which more lawlike regularities can be derived, in comparative rankings and ratings to further divide the facts of our data, and to more carefully define the exact meanings of the theoretical words in our language. One example of this would be ordering and classification of ego functions and the clarification of the time of onset and definition of the same. Such classifications are said to be needed for diagnostic differentiation as well as for therapeutic intervention. But the ultimate goal is to raise the scientific position of psychoanalysis by way of formalism or exactness.

A recent book entitled *Freud's Unfinished Journey* (Breger, 1981) is devoted to an examination of the idea that Freud was a transitional figure between the values of nineteenth and early twentieth century western society and thus between very different perspectives of world views. It has a provocative chapter entitled "Psychoanalysis is not Science." The book as a whole is not exactly revolutionary and this chapter is more representative of many such endeavors than it is innovative. Essentially it says that science is objective, aims at gaining truths, develops general principals and laws, and has a world view that encompasses these features. Psychoanalysis on the other hand is subjective, has a personal criterion of truth, enjoys general principles that are guidelines rather than laws, and presents a world view that is a uniquely new endeavor involving the development of personal paradigms. The author's conclusion is that psychoanalysis is an art which is similar to other arts but is also much more than them. It is unique; a philosophy, a system of values, and even an approach to life. All in all, psychoanalysis is terribly precious.

Such a point of view, which is by no means an unpopular one, not only allows for a marvelous feeling of specialness but it is also accompanied by a certain license granted to us as artists. We can scoff at theory. We can beg off explanations by pleading that certain things are beyond words, and we can be imprecise in our teaching. It is not a license easily to be allowed to expire. Indeed it has developed into a subschool of analytic practice that is a polar opposite in the range that starts with the formalists.

At this end of the spectrum are those analysts who eschew all theory and who urge us but to listen to the patient, to enter the patient's world, and to never impose our theories on the patient. Such an approach betrays either naiveté or a suspect honesty. If a patient tells us that his life's troubles are due to demons, we may listen as empathically as possible and try mightily to ascertain the hidden meaning of such demons to the patient, but above all else, we simply do not believe a demon theory of neurogenesis. We simply cannot survive without a personal theory to sift the facts as we hear them; and soon we turn to some new and fundamental facts about science that may enable us to bridge the gap between the so-called subjectivity of hermeneutics and the objectivity of natural science. This gap has been bridged in past years by an accumulation of studies into the way science really works. These investigations are inspired by philosophers of science who sought to free themselves from the shackles of this natural science formalism without falling into the random freedom assigned by art. The answer to the dilemma lies in what is called the postempiricist account of natural science and it contains the following points (Hesse, 1978, p. 172).

1. All the data of science are derived in the light of theories, that is, the theory tells you what to see and what to hear.
2. Theories are not models external to nature but are the facts themselves.
3. The lawlike relations are internal because facts are constituted by their interrelations with one another.
4. The language of natural science is inexact and formalized only at the cost of distortion.
5. Meanings are determined by theory and not by correspondence with the facts.

Now anyone who studies these points will soon see that they are the very points that psychoanalysis and hermeneutics have often faced as accusations. But these points are now the *backbone* of all of those natural sciences that we have often hoped to emulate and that we felt we have fallen short of. We soon come around to the astounding fact that to some extent all of our science rests on interpretation and that physics can join psychoanalysis as a hermeneutic discipline. Physicists interpret the traces of high energy particles according to their preconceived theoretical notions, and there is no observation in physics or in analysis that is free of theory.

The interpretation of texts either in literature or in the experiments of physics is, of course, different from that of dialogue. The hermeneutic approach to a fixed text allows the reader to bring his fund of knowledge and beliefs to what is written so that there is never a resolution as to what the author really meant or the experiment revealed. Rather, different readings at different times will yield different interpretations. On the other hand, in a dialogue with another person we discover an exchange of meanings, with each participant offering a personal theory and a personal set of meanings. Such an exchange is resolvable only through a process of negotiation and this is more or less what we see in the psychoanalytic process; patient and analyst seek to determine the patient's life story by way of interpretation, with the latter word never standing for a fixed revelation but rather a negotiated translation. It has, of course, as we have noticed, been quite difficult to handle the metaphoric and fluid quality of the words and sentences that make up the psychoanalytic discourse within the framework of the usual forms of scientific investigation. The decline of the positivistic outlook in science, however, did not bring ready relief to the status of psychoanalysis because one still had to struggle with the enormous problems posed by the seeming lack of replicability of our data, as well as the lack of consensus as to what it meant. However, over the years we have seen that many scientific enterprises were equally caught up in discovering that interpretation of any data depends on the investigator, the theory he is using, and the interests he has in mind. Scientists were forced to see that it is relatively easy to examine fixed, closed systems in order to gain replicability and consensus, but that once one considers open systems studied by investigators with special motives and interests who discover things that had heretofore been hidden, then the simpler forms of scientific methodology are found wanting. My own conclusion is that the hermeneutic approach is part and parcel of all scientific activity.

This is not to say that physics and psychoanalysis are similar scientific enterprises since the differences are enormous, but it is to say that science is science and thus uses a variety of methods and procedures to unlock the secrets of the world. It is also to say that we must stop being preoccupied with the seemingly special status of psychoanalysis. To insist that our discipline is so unique and different that it is like no other science, or is really an art form, is a dangerous retreat that robs us of the opportunities to reach succeeding generations of analysts. I suspect that Ricoeur (1970), who was so right about the hermeneutic essentials of psychoanalysis, tended to reinforce this special status position, and that others rightfully objected to it. However, I cannot see how psychoanalysis can be other than a hermeneutic discipline, since the bread and butter of our science is interpretation. To argue the point that there is much besides interpretation that goes on in analysis is to confuse the setting with the process and to confuse the phases of understanding and explanation. Prolonged understanding may set the stage but it is only half the story. As long as we commit ourselves to a depth psychology then we are bound only by the methods we employ that are essentially psychological, and thus we must always *interpret* the holding environment, or soothing object or whatever to the patient and to ourselves.

We, of course, do not choose one theory over the other on the basis of faith alone. Nor can we say that one perspective is "closer to reality" than any other, since such a judgment would require us to be able to see reality "as it is." But the exchangeability of theory seemingly does not allow this. We do, however, belong to a tradition of empiricism which insists that faiths must be judged by evidence not under their control; that is, evidence must not be interpreted by proponents of the faiths to the point where it is forced to confirm the faith in question (Gellner, 1974). The supposed incommensurability of theory or the inability to translate one theory with another (Goldberg, 1985) does not mean that theories cannot be compared. Without a commitment to the thesis that one theory is closer to reality than another, we *can* say that one theory is better than another.

Not only do we use criteria of coherence, comprehensiveness, and consistency, but we always rely on a pragmatic criterion of getting farther, understanding more, and advancing our science. If the structural model of the mind does the job then there is no reason to forsake it. But if it seems to harbor contradictions or to need heroic stretching to accommodate clinical material, then there is every reason, even necessity, to examine alternate ways of seeing the psychological world.

If we join or rejoin the ranks of science then we have a further obligation; namely, to cease our arguments about who is right. At many stages of scientific progress we witness a plurality of theories, and we use them all in a pragmatic way without a clear vision of truth except within the confines of the theory. For a while, everyone is right. If the day comes that a new theory supersedes an old one, it will only be on the basis of continuing dialogues which aim to promote understanding and to clear away misunderstanding, and that, of course, is the fundamental message of hermeneutics.

SELF PSYCHOLOGY AND THE MODELING OF THE MIND

Self psychology began as an effort to expand psychoanalysis in order to allow consideration of an analytic approach to a certain subset of psychopathology: the narcissistic personality disorders. As such it asked us to look at the world of and about these patients, in a manner different from the ways in which we had looked before; that is no more than any model or theory asks of us. Once we do so, we gather different data and necessarily see a different world. Such a new perception seems at times to offend some people, but putting that aside for a moment, it seems to be the case that every new model or theory will be at odds with the previous ones. That is what progress in science is all about. Thus self psychology, by definition, will yield a new set of facts, new lawlike relations, and new conclusions. Whether they will be true or correct or illusory is another question, and I am postponing testing that point for now.

The crux of the model of self psychology is that of the selfobject, that is, another person experienced as part of oneself in a functional manner, that travels a developmental road from archaic to mature. Selfobjects are universal, ubiquitous, and enduring. Selfobject transferences, in turn, are the fundamental features of the clinical theory. And it naturally follows from what we have said, that one must know what to look for in order to see a selfobject transference; and that one must, to put it bluntly, believe in them in order to see them. The motto is, "I wouldn't have seen it, if I hadn't believed it." Unless we allow ourselves this manner of discovery we will never find anything in our clinical material that will allow us to go beyond what is the tried and true, and thus we will always rediscover "eternal truths."

The development, working through, and resolution of selfobject transferences is the core of the practice of psychoanalytic self psychology. The first such transferences were outlined by Kohut as corresponding to developmental stages of grandiosity and idealization and were accordingly named as mirror transferences or those assigned to the grandiose self, and idealizing ones, or those assigned to the idealized parental imago. In keeping with the spirit of an inquiring science, a third selfobject transference, the twinship or alter ego, was later added by Kohut. Perhaps more will be discovered someday. These transferences arise spontaneously in any well-conducted treatment or analysis and certainly are not fostered or encouraged by any active behavior of the therapist. Inasmuch as no one was aware of or described any sort of transferences before Freud pointed them out, it comes as no surprise that selfobject transferences will remain equally opaque to the uninformed novice. The method employed by self psychology, that of empathy, to gain access to the data of the clinical setting, is the same as that employed by any and all depth psychologies. The debate and confusion about that much-abused word, I think, stems from its popular and common definition associated with some sort of emotional resonance. Self psychology stands with all scientific inquiry in considering empathy as the only route to another person's inner world. Of course all empathy must be guided by a theory and/or a model, and only in this sense is self psychology deviant from inquiries employing other models. Utilizing the self-selfobject model in one or another of its transference manifestations, we hope to perceive the psychological state of another person. I cannot imagine how that differs from the stance of any and all depth psychological efforts save for the particular model that one subscribes to as best explaining the data. I think we stand together as investigators of the inner world of man, and we thereby all employ empathic immersion in the internal world of others. External observation is, of course, never discounted, but it is always subsumed under the question of "what it must feel like" to be tall or fat or have an accent or wear shabby clothes or whatever. Such observations are not in opposition to empathy but are a natural part of the primary question directed to our understanding of another person's life experience.

CLINICAL EXAMPLE

I would like to present a brief clinical vignette to launch what I hope will be a clarification of my main thesis about self psychology, namely, that it includes all of the usual features of psychoanalysis but adds the self-selfobject transference in an effort to broaden and expand our vision. In the words of Albert Einstein: "No fairer destiny could be allotted to any [physical] theory than that it should itself point out the way to introducing a more comprehensive theory in which it lives on as a limiting case." Conflict in this view is thus of secondary importance and follows self-selfobject failures or disruptions. But self psychology is not to be thought of as dispensing with conflict. Rather it says that one must have attained a developmental level of a certain self-integrity *in order* to engage in conflict. Weak, en-feebled, or fragmenting selves are primarily engaged in this initial task of self-cohesion.

My case is not really mine since it was presented to me in consultation by a very experienced therapist who was having difficulty with his patient, a 40-year-old depressed woman who had been in psychotherapy twice a week for about a year. This therapist was not the first one for the patient, but he had been the most successful; although he was quite aware of periodic episodes that were filled with accusations by the patient to the effect that the therapy was of little help to her. Her therapist could only endure these periods with mixed feelings of help-lessness and guilt. There was little doubt that the patient seemed to profit from her treatment overall, and she and the therapist seemed resigned to letting these periods of anger and discon-tent just "spend themselves" rather than hope for a quick res-olution. No effort of his to pinpoint the onset and/or to explain it seemed to be rewarded.

The therapist presented the history and treatment of the patient to me in some detail. I shall not repeat them here since the crucial question that we needed to attend to was, what went wrong when the patient felt so misunderstood and abandoned. Essentially hers was a life of fairly good achievement mingled with a chronic discontent at missing out. The latter was evi-denced in terms of men, money, beauty, and so on. I must underscore the fact that the therapist was sensitive and aware of self psychological issues and was convinced of some failures on his part, ones that he innocently repeated. He told me of the latest such disruptive event. The patient had gone off on a holiday, and she told of spending a day of shopping with a friend. She had succeeded in working out her feelings about this by herself and explained them to the therapist, who agreed with her but added that more work was still needed. This was the point at which the patient got upset, and the same seemed true, soon thereafter, of the therapist. I suggested to him that he seemed, at the moment, to take away an achievement on the part of the patient. He next reported one of the patient's dreams to me, one that she had successfully interpreted, and which he had likewise joined with her in agreement. Enthusiastically he proceeded to expand his agreement with one point that needed elaboration, and once again the patient had felt deflated and angry. The therapist felt less that he was competing with the patient and more that primarily he was eager to do more for her. I felt that she was clearly asking him to admire and accept what she had to offer without in any way indicating that it was deficient or inadequate or in need of expansion. She needed a selfobject response of mirroring or acceptance, while the therapist's need to "have the last word" effectively stymied the patient's effort. Once made aware of this, the therapist was able to utilize it with great effectiveness, and he so notified me in a letter some weeks later. The disruptions became less frequent, but, more importantly, they became capable of being understood.

This brief account is the sort of material that allows multiple forms of explanation and/or interpretation. I, myself, had also listened to the story with a model involving penis envy: one that centered around a depressed and angry woman forever resentful for not having what others had and seeking redress from a therapist who could never fulfill her desires. I had long ago found my own discontent with the penis envy model, but had discovered an interesting exercise to see how generations of analysts had handled their own reactions to its failings. The best one I discovered is that of penis envy as a metaphor. The claim was that Freud did not mean penis envy to be a real issue of deprivation and envy but rather one that covered a host of such negative affective experiences. Of course, this not only does a disservice to Freud, who clearly meant it to be a reality, but it also highlights the historical point that we cling to models beyond their usefulness both in time and and in terms of applicability. If now we can offer a model that does a better job of explaining a familiar form of clinical data, then perhaps we are on the road of answering the question that I raised earlier: How do we know what is the best or correct or true explanation?

My second case is of a long analysis, and again is one that I must unfortunately summarize beyond the form that allows for easy comprehension. It is that of a woman who had had an earlier analysis, one that centered on these very same issues of deprivation, envy, and depression. She felt much benefited from that first analysis, but her depression seemed unrelenting, and this caused her to seek further treatment. She was a most willing and cooperative patient but she soon evidenced a trait that became quite central to the analysis: she was a clock watcher to the very second. A clock with a sweep second hand sits to the side of my desk, and this patient would scrutinize it at the beginning and end of each hour. She was quite ashamed of her intense concentration on the time, but it soon managed to grow into a discussion of intense rage at being cheated, of a few seconds, and her equally intense joy at being gifted, again with a short period of time. We managed to see this as a focus for all her feelings about being given an unfair shake by fate, and we also connected it to alternating experiences of deprivation and overindulgence by her parents. The work of such treatment is no doubt familiar to most therapists and analysts who can probably also equally recognize and share my own feelings of wanting to do more for her, of resentment at not being appreciated for all that I had done, and of helplessness at the seeming intractability of her conviction of life's unfairness.

The bedrock of this and, indeed, every woman's search for fulfillment is, for most analysts, always some variation on the theme of resignation with an occasional foray into substitution; that is, the baby for the penis. Self psychology urges us to go beyond the Oedipal conflicts that are played out in this kind of analysis, and thus it allowed me a modicum of hope, of enthusiasm, and of curiosity. In the transference one could see the patient's handling of the interpretation of her dreams as always falling short—always seeming to need me to add the final word. However, now and again she would allow herself to successfully analyze a dream in its entirety, and sensing my approval, in that I had nothing to add, she would evidence a certain kind of excitement and pleasure that seemed either totally new or else a reawakening of a long forgotten affective state. Now the emergence of the patient's repressed ambition and grandiosity appeared, and with it the need for a selfobject of acknowledgement, acceptance, and admiration. It should not be necessary to assure you that none of this is acted out by the therapist or analyst. Rather, as in the first case, we interpret after our failures since success needs no acclamation.

This patient's entry into a mirroring selfobject transference effectively removed the preoccupation with envy and sadness and replaced it with excitement and fear of overstimulation. Now the supposed penis envy could be seen as related to the failure of the depressed mother to wholeheartedly respond to the child's achievement, coupled with the preoccupied, but not depressed father who insisted on his own recognition from his children. This certainly is similar to the little girl's disappointment at her shortcomings, but the selfobject model sees it in a matrix of relationships with others who affirm or enforce our self-perceptions. Such selfobjects are really functioning parts of ourselves, since we never achieve a feeling of pride without first traversing the road of others who are proud of us. My patient had not had such a developmental achievement in childhood, and analysis was a belated effort to effect such a development. It was not an effort to undo the conflicts that arose from her frustrated drives, because the use of the self-selfobject model allowed us to go deeper, to explain more, and to be more effective. And as such it could lay claim to being true, correct, and better—until, of course, a still better model came along. The patient analyzed her own dreams and utilized the established selfobject transference to internalize a change from the intense and unbearable overexcitement of accomplishment to a more sustainable and tolerable sense of proper fulfillment. She no longer needed to have the extra time, since she no longer needed to envy what I had. Only when I failed as a mirroring selfobject—much as did my enthusiastic colleague who came for supervision for his need to do more—only then, did the derailment of the transference need to be interpreted.

I suppose one could say that this patient's feeling of power and control over me in the analysis, particularly of her dreams, allowed her to have a fantasized penis and thus a magical feeling of repair. But such a last-ditch stand, an insistence on the validity of classical psychoanalysis, fails to live up to clinical validation, since self psychologists are hardly naive and duped at every turn. More importantly, self psychologists insist on not treating the patient as adversary; as someone out to belittle or devalue or gain some advantage over the therapist. That is a posture that is not only morally offensive, but is probably primarily self-serving and designed to allow all sorts of therapeutic misbehavior. Most significantly, the posture is unnecessary, since our models are tools and not truth bearers. They do not need to explain everything, but rather they should be used, as any tool, to fit the need and the occasion. How well they fit becomes the determinant of their correctness.

DISCUSSION

There are both immediate and far-reaching effects of the self psychological approach to clinical material. For one, we are forced to reexamine our views about normal growth, development, especially the problem of the development of the self. Our analytic colleagues' work on infant observation is amazingly congenial with the model of self-selfobject theory. As an aside, I must say that we still employ vicarious introspection in our data gathering; a laughing or crying baby is judged by our own experiences with those states, and we do not count muscle twitches or take blood pressure readings to determine the existence of such emotional experiences. To move forward a bit, I can also say that an incredible amount of clarity has been introduced to the entire field of adolescent psychology, by an appreciation of the need for certain forms of sustaining selfobjects during that trying period. Another jump brings us to aging and the profound need for selfobjects to enable us to maintain our integrity and fulfill our goals during that developmental period. I personally have found that a rich addition to the treatment of the dying patient is offered by the use of the self-selfobject model, especially in the comprehension of the terrible fear of total abandonment that is so crucial for those individuals.

The concept of the developmental line of selfobjects from archaic to mature enables us to consider the nature of such relationships at each of life's signal points of growth. The selfobjects needs of an infant for mirroring will, of course, be significantly different from those of a lecturer before an audience. They will differ in a variety of ways ranging from the urgency, the need to control, and the flexibility of change. But a mature selfobject relationship is just as necessary to sustain the self as is an infantile one. We never dispense with the need for selfobjects. We never achieve an independence that is free from selfobjects, but rather one that has a mature capacity to utilize them. This, essentially, is the message of our therapy and the working through process: to allow development to proceed to an optimal relationship with one's selfobjects.

Psychoanalytic self psychology also demands a recasting of much of classical psychoanalysis that is posited on theories of drive discharge vis-à-vis a mental apparatus. This is hardly the fault of self psychology, however, since our theory has so long been under attack: from its outmoded energy concepts to its failure to account for the open exchange of, and with social and cultural systems. For example, a powerful new insight seems available to us in our study of certain forms of cults based on the archaic need to merge with messianic or charismatic idealized figures. No doubt analysis has always offered us explanations of sorts for these issues; but it has never been totally satisfactory, and it has often been terribly reductionistic. The entire problem of the development of the self awaits our further work in theory construction, and such work may offer a most hoped for articulation with the other sciences of man.

Psychoanalytic self psychology offers us a new tool to employ in our work. Only the prolonged use of a tool allows one to determine its value and worth. Only the proper use of a tool allows one to judge its personal advantages. Anyone who first attempts to use a tool, or a model, will necessarily experience frustration and anger and, perhaps, will condemn it as useless and worthless and sometimes even as bad. This is not an indulgence that analysts or indeed any scientist can afford. As a representative of psychoanalytic self psychology I suppose I am attempting to sell it to you, but am also in the most fortunate position of asking you to try it out for as long as you like—and then it is yours.

Chapter 6

Object Relations Theory

Arnold H. Modell, M.D.

We are asked to illustrate the schema or model that influences how we actually work as clinicians. It may be a bit pretentious to refer to this schema as a model for I doubt that it is so fully fleshed out or articulated. It is rather a question of our basic assumptions and the traditions that claim our loyalty. All of this is, of course, filtered through our own personalities, so that I do not feel that I can represent the "school" of object relations theory whatever that may be, but I can describe what has influenced me, what the underlying assumptions of object relations theory are, and how they may differ from other parallel traditions.

I have been most influenced by the work of Winnicott and to a lesser extent by the contributions of Fairbairn and Balint. Fairbairn (1952) has suggested that libido is essentially object seeking; I have modified this aphorism to state that affects are essentially object seeking (Modell, 1975). This brings into view an area of clinical experience that is not ordinarily encompassed by classical instinct theory—the problem of relatedness. If affects are object seeking then true relatedness (in contrast to compliance) is characterized by the communication of genuine affects; or to state it in the obverse, nonrelatedness is characterized by the noncommunication of affects or the communication of false or misleading affects. Balint has taught us the importance of dependency, that psychoanalytic therapy "is essentially an object relationship; [that] all the events which lead ultimately to therapeutic change in the patient's mind are initiated by events happening in a two-person relationship, i.e., happening essentially *between* two people and not inside only one of them" (Balint, 1968, p. 9). All three—Balint, Winnicott, and Fairbairn—although they differ significantly, share in the recognition of the importance of dependency. For Winnicott, regression in the analytic situation was defined simply as regression to dependency, and Fairbairn (1952) has emphasized that dependency is not confined to childhood, that there is such a thing as "mature dependency."

However, in other respects Winnicott and Balint need to be distinguished from Fairbairn in terms of Fairbairn's emphasis upon the internal object. There are, of course, basically two object relations theories; for the term *object relationship* could mean relationship to an inner or an outer object. This distinction does separate the Kleinians and Fairbairn, who pay special attention to the inner object, from those of us who pay special attention to the outer, that is to say, the actual object; what Winnicott described as the facilitating environment. But this outer object is not necessarily coincident with what is "objectively" real.

Although Fairbairn followed Klein in his focus upon internal objects, unlike Melanie Klein he did not believe in an impulse or instinct psychology: "the distinction between the id and ego is abolished and the ego is regarded as an original structure which is itself the source of impulse-tension" (Fairbairn, 1952, p. 157). Kernberg's (1975) contributions to object relations theory are, in my opinion, in part derived from this Kleinian-Fairbairn tradition but modified by contemporary ego psychology. The work of Bion (1970) in some measure diminished the distance that separated the Kleinian group and other object relations theorists. Bion, through his interest in group psychology, has introduced as a potential focus a consideration of a two-person psychology: "A science of relationships has yet to be established and one would look to find some discipline analogous to mathematics to represent the relationship of one element in the structure of the psychic personality with another" (Bion, 1970, p. 53).

As I have said, Winnicott paid special attention to the actual object to the extent that he found himself saying (1965) that: "There is no such thing as an infant." There are, I believe, radical conclusions to be drawn from this view of child development. The principle conclusion is that we are in the realm of a two-person and not a one-person psychology. In a certain sense Melanie Klein's position is the more classical, with her emphasis upon the internalized object which permits her to maintain the classical intrapsychic stance of psychoanalysis. I would not depreciate the importance of internalized objects, but the internalized object and the actual object are not equivalent concepts and we cannot evade the problem by describing actual objects by a notational system of object representations. What occurs in a relationship between two people is not simply something that can be described in the mind of the subject.

This acknowledgment of the importance of the actual object has led to an appreciation of the importance of the analytic setting itself and to the role of the analyst as part of this setting. These observations were in a sense forced upon us through the treatment of the more seriously ill patient, but I do believe that the principles learned there are applicable to the less seriously ill patient as well. What I am considering here is the broad matter of environmental failures, or more precisely environmental impingements. The parental environment is a buffer between the child and the dangers in the external world, and through their affective responses the parental caretakers are also mediators between the child and his own internal world. There are all manner of degrees of failure in this process from the massive to the subtle. These failures lead to a "freezing" of the traumatic situation, a developmental arrest if you will, which is then reactivated in the therapeutic relationship. To acknowledge the influence of trauma at the hands of the "actual" object in the etiology of psychopathology does not minimize the importance of the subjectively created object. Object relations theorists such as Winnicott have not suggested any simplistic equation correlating environmental trauma with psychopathological outcome. Winnicott preferred the term *impingement* to describe that which interferes with psychic development. The impingement may be environmental, but not necessarily so, for the strength of the instincts may also be experienced as an impingement. It is a term that does not prejudge the outcome, for impingements may also have a positive potential depending upon the individual's response.

I believe that I have said nothing that could not be accepted by most "classical" analysts. What then is the claim for a special point of view of object relations theory?

We assume that in health or relative health certain things can be taken for granted; normally, certain processes occur silently and become noisy only when something is missing. In a certain group of patients the relationship between the patient and the therapist can move silently, and in this sense be taken for granted. An examination of the history of psychoanalytic technique may make this point more explicit. A very careful reading of Freud's account of his treatment of the Rat Man (Lipton, 1977) has, in my opinion at least, demonstrated that Freud did take this relationship for granted. For this reason he was able to invite the Rat Man to share that famous piece of herring without having to think that this represented a breach of technique; Freud considered this as part of the nontechnical relationship with the patient, a part of the ordinary physicianly relationship which of course may lead to transference associations which would then come under the purview of psychoanalytic technique.

Those who are influenced by object relations theory tend to have acquired experiences with more seriously ill patients and hence do not take this nontechnical relationship, that is, the patients relating to us as a physician or a therapist, for granted. When there has been a significant failure on the part of the parental caretakers, to entrust oneself to the therapeutic process becomes intensely conflictual. This absence of trust is truly an absence; that is, it is something that is missing, and it can produce, as we all know, a great deal of noise. So for some patients the setting of the analysis, which includes the relationship to the analyst, is of the utmost importance. One may place all of this under the heading of transference. As in other forms of transference the working of the repetition compulsion is certainly in evidence, but, and this is where the assumptions of object relations theory enter in a way that significantly influences technique, issues of safety are conceptually of a different order as compared to the transference neurosis which has the Oedipus complex at its center. Toward the end of his life Freud (1940) said, in "An Outline of Psychoanalysis": "Just as the id is directed exclusively to obtaining pleasure, so the ego is governed by considerations of safety. The ego has set itself up the task of self-preservation, which the id appears to neglect" (p. 199). Joseph Sandler (1960), has elaborated this idea from the standpoint of ego psychology with his felicitous concept of "the background of safety." Object relations theory approaches this issue from a somewhat different direction, that of the parent–child interaction. I have said that these two forms of transference are of a conceptually different order. We do not have any ready-made way of placing these differences within an overall organizing conceptual framework such as was once provided by instinct theory. But my point may be understood better if I recall Freud's earlier distinction between the instincts of self-preservation, which he termed *ego instincts*, and the more commonly recognized sexual instincts. Object relations theory, to borrow from this antiquated terminology, covers the area of the instincts of self-preservation as it describes the primary protective object or objects that stand between the self and the external world of early childhood. This need for a protective object is something which we never fully outgrow, even though we know the protection to be illusory. Contemporary biology does not give much support for the concept of instinct: instead it describes attachment behavior (Bowlby, 1969), which is understood to be a conceptually distinct and separate system from sexual behavior.

Winnicott (1954) said: "The setting of analysis reproduces the early and earliest mothering techniques. It invites regression by reason of its reliability." Winnicott's reference to regression may have obscured the fact that what is re-created in the setting of analysis is not a regression in the sense of the transference transporting the patient back to the first years of life, which is nonsensical, but a *symbolic* re-creation of aspects of early mother–child reaction. This view I believe, has profound implications for a model of the mind. It questions whether the achievement of self/object differentiation is developmentally analogous to psychosexual stages with its sequential points of closure. This traditional view can be likened to a wedding cake model with its hierarchical levels analogous to archaeological strata. *The model that I am suggesting implies that issues concerning autonomy and self/object differentiation are carried forward and are worked through symbolically during the entire life cycle.*

The capacity to perceive and to experience symbolic equivalents is a profoundly human characteristic. We know that what the analyst does as an analyst without the introduction of any active measures, that is, without "parameters," is symbolic of certain caretaking functions. We understand that this psychoanalytic activity symbolically re-creates the "holding" that occurs between a mother and a child. Many aspects of ordinary "good" technique can be experienced by the patient as symbolic equivalents of aspects of the parent–child relationship (Modell, 1976). This includes the fact that the analyst or therapist (and I here refer also to analytically informed long-term psychotherapy) is constant, reliable, primarily there for the patient's needs, has a more benign, less critical judgment than the patient, is empathically capable of enabling the patient to feel understood, and is able to clarify what is bewildering or frightening. This symbolic "holding" also means setting limits, analogous to holding a child who is having a temper tantrum, and accepting what is obnoxious as a mother accepts a child's soiling. The fact that the therapist continues to function as a therapist is also a symbolic assurance that he or she has not been damaged. I have noted that the holding environment is also symbolic of the acceptance of what is obnoxious. For example, a patient in analysis who believed that the mother could not accept soiling avoided washing and confronted the analyst with an almost intolerable body odor. This piece of obnoxious behavior was at first accepted without comment but later became the focus of a significant confrontation in the context of this apparent repetition compulsion. What is significant here from the standpoint of object relations theory is not only that a piece of the interaction between mother and child is repeated in the transference, but that the analyst is in fact a new object and offers the possibility of a different resolution. Loewald (1980) has said, "I say new discovery of objects, and not discovery of new objects, because the essence of such new object-relationships is the opportunity they offer for rediscovery of the early paths of the development of object-relations, leading to a new way of relating to objects as well as of being and relating to oneself. This new discovery of oneself and of objects, this reorganization of ego and objects, is made possible by the encounter with a new object" (p. 225).

The therapeutic setting leads to an illusion that the therapist stands as a protective barrier between the self and the dangers of both the internal and external world. This illusion of connectedness carries within it the seeds of its own disillusion, for it contains an implicit denial of separateness, so that an eventual confrontation with reality will occur if treatment persists. The therapeutic setting and the therapist's activities, in addition to being perceived as a holding environment, also become the stage upon which conflicts concerning self/object differentiation and autonomy are symbolically actualized, so that early developmental stages are symbolically recreated. Unlike the transference neurosis with its highly idiosyncratic content, there is a marked uniformity to its content which is consistent with developmental issues. For example, in accordance with the stage of illusory merging there is an implicit belief that the patient can be understood without having to make an effort to communicate, that a cure can be effected by mere contiguity with the therapist, that there is no need to be active on one's own behalf. To take responsibility for oneself is an acknowledgement of separateness. The details of these manifestations need not concern us; I wish only to illustrate that the therapist's activity as a therapist becomes symbolically invested with the conflicts of individuation. The patient unconsciously draws us into this drama so that we are not merely a screen to receive projections but an actor whose actions promote a symbolic working through. To understand this drama we require a two-person object-related schema that acknowledges, as Winnicott said, that early and earliest mother–child interactions are recreated in the analytic setting.

There is implicit in the foregoing description a question of the range of application of object relations theory. Conflicts concerning self/object differentiation and conflicts concerning autonomy, with the attendant wishes to control the object absolutely, do not comprise all of the content of psychotherapy or psychoanalysis.

I do not minimize the importance of psychosexual conflict and the Oedipus complex, the vicissitudes of which lead to a nearly infinite variety of neurotic content. However, there is a certain group of patients that we have come to describe as narcissistic, for whom problems of autonomy of the self and conflicts concerning self/object differentiation will occupy a major portion of their treatment. There are others for whom these issues will be prominent in the opening phase when the therapist is yet to be trusted, only to recede and become a secondary or background theme. And finally there is a third group in whom issues concerning object relations never enter overtly into the psychopathology. Here object relations theory makes a conceptual but not a technical contribution; I do not think that I would conduct the therapy or psychoanalysis of such individuals differently from my colleagues who have a more classical point of view; but I would think differently regarding the question of how treatment works.

In the narcissistic group the object relations model of the mind will, I believe, influence what we actually do. If one accepts the use of the therapeutic relationship as a holding environment that will allow for the symbolic recapitulation of early developmental stages, one will learn to wait (in some instances a very long time indeed) as both Winnicott (1965) and Balint (1968) advised, and guard against intruding, especially by means of deep interpretations. I have come to accept a further technical principle: issues of safety take precedence and must be attended to before the derivatives of the Oedipus complex. (Gedo [1979] has also emphasized that early developmental conflicts are not necessarily regressive evasions of Oedipal conflict.) There is frequently a matter of choice, as content relating to safety and content derived from the Oedipus complex may and frequently do coexist. What I am referring to is the problem of entrustment. Most experienced therapists recognize that at the beginning of treatment there is an implicit question of entrustment and safety. For some this can be taken for granted (as part of the initial "confident transference"), for others it can remain a central issue and may require years of preparatory work to enable the patient to feel safe enough to be spontaneous. It is in this sense that I believe that issues of safety take precedence over Oedipal content.

Although Winnicott did not write about technique in a systematic fashion, one can discern in his work several clear and explicit therapeutic principles. For Winnicott, I believe, would share Freud's view of the aims of psychoanalytic therapy as creating a condition so that "where id was so ego shall be." But Winnicott viewed this as a means to a further end, this end being the establishment of sufficient ego growth to permit the emergence of the maximum spontaneity of the self. Analysis cannot proceed in the face of a false or compliant transference nor can it proceed without true spontaneity. For Winnicott, paradoxically, freedom or spontaneity of the self was not possible without some boundary or constraint; in this sense the analytic setting itself could be viewed as such a boundary.

(There may be some overlap here with Bion's [1970] concept of the container and the contained.) As a corollary, if one is able to achieve a situation of maximum spontaneity, there is also the potential for maximum destructiveness within this boundary of constraint. For Winnicott this destructiveness was not understood as a derivative of the death instinct but had in itself a positive potential: "Without the experience of maximum destructiveness (object not protected) the subject never places the analyst outside the area of omnipotent control" (Winnicott, 1971, p. 91). In order to learn from the therapeutic experience, in order to take something in, there must be some limitation in the belief in one's own omnipotence and omniscience. Further, the capacity for symbolic illusion upon which therapy rests may have a similar foundation. The clinical vignette that follows illustrates this principle.

Most of our patients have some capacity to make use of the therapeutic relationship. The absence of such a capacity in a person considered to be a possible candidate for psychoanalysis is quite unusual. But, occasionally people present themselves to us as patients who are unable to make use of either psychotherapy or psychoanalysis. This group has been described by Joyce McDougall (1980) as antianalysands. She described a group of patients who accommodate themselves to the external setting of the analytic situation but do not make use of the *process:* the patient talks but nothing seems to be happening because something essential is missing. (It is like the absent organ which we occasionally encounter in nature.) And since we learn most from our failures, I plan to present a clinical vignette of just such a treatment failure.

After 2½ years of work with a professional man in his middle thirties his analysis was interrupted by mutual consent. The analysis was judged by both of us to be a complete and total failure. Although the analysis was in difficulty from the outset, I thought that there would be some nonspecific therapeutic gain that warranted our continuing. At first I could not quite believe the patient's claim that he obtained absolutely nothing from the analysis, but later I reluctantly came to agree with him that this was unfortunately true.

There was in this case a major failure of the early holding environment, which, for reasons that are still unclear, appeared to have been decisive. In order to go to work, his mother left him at the age of two in the care of an elderly blind grandfather who spoke only Yiddish, which the patient did not understand. We know of others who have suffered an analogous trauma and who yet remain open and give the world a second chance; but for reasons which I do not understand this did not occur here. It was as if he turned his back on the world in a total and profound fashion. This rejection was covered over by a false self-organization that allowed him to be superficially friendly and amiable. As we shall see he was completely unable to learn from experience because he retained an inner system of thought and being completely uninfluenced by the outside world; that is, a system under his own omnipotent control. This man was not in any sense clinically psychotic, although some may call this a private psychosis. I gradually came to recognize that he had a fundamental incapacity to take anything in, that is, to learn from experience. This was true despite a high intelligence. There would be occasional moments in the analysis when he would appear to be free associating and material would emerge, especially from dreams, that was relevant and promising. But invariably I found the work I had thought we had done to be transitory in nature. We had been writing in sand, nothing stuck, and nothing was retained. It appeared that the capacity for illusory transformation of objects, that is, their symbolic transformation, was absent. McDougall (1980) has also observed the meager use of metaphor in these cases. The patient did not really believe in an inner psychic life or what we call psychic reality; to say that he was not psychologically minded would be an understatement; he had virtually no curiosity regarding his own inner life. He knew I believed in some inner psychic reality but he saw this as a type of religious conviction, perhaps something inculcated in my psychoanalytic training.

This belief of mine intrigued him as something he wished he had, but at bottom he thought either I was faking it or I was deluded.

Instead of genuine learning (taking something in and making it his own), his learning was quick, superficial, and shallow. He picked up information from the air so to speak, he was "au courant" with all the latest stylish professional jargon, catchwords that he picked up from conversations and skimming professional journals. He achieved his professional credentials by cramming for examinations and was very skillful at multiple choice questions. But he rightly felt himself to be an imposter, for nothing stuck to him. Early in the analysis he informed me that he never completed a book that was not required as a school assignment; I dismissed this at first as an exaggeration but later learned that it was literally true. However, he did have, perhaps as a compensation, a remarkable capacity for retaining trivia. He knew the complete lyrics to a large number of popular songs, and instead of free associating would recite the words, which often enough did have a certain tangential, though pre-structured, relevance.

Many of his human relationships had this same superficial, banal quality. The shallowness of his relationships is seen in his inability or unwillingness to experience psychic pain, so that he could not mourn those that he lost, but also he could not experience pleasure; he lived a form of psychic death. He had been married before I knew him but had divorced his wife primarily because he felt bored with her. He remarried, hoping that his second wife would bring him, as he hoped the analysis would, some sense of psychic aliveness.

What was absent, like an absent organ, was what Winnicott described as the capacity to make use of an object. This capacity combines the ability to learn from the experience with another, to accept a certain modicum of psychic pain that is associated with the possibility of loss or destruction of the object. But what was most important, he lacked a capacity to make use of illusion, to transform a relationship symbolically.

The capacity to learn from others requires at bottom plac-ing the object, in Winnicott's language (1969), "outside the area of omnipotent control." Winnicott pointed to a significant dif-ference between genuine and superficial relating correspond-ing to the distinctions between the true and false self; you will recall this group of which my patient is an example may main-tain themselves within the therapeutic *situation* but do not make use of the *process*. Winnicott (1971) has described it as follows:

> In the sequence one can say that first there is object-re-lating, then in the end there is object-use; in between, however, is the most difficult thing, perhaps, in human development; or the most irksome of all the early failures that come for mending. This thing that there is in between relating and use is the subject's placing of the object outside the area of the subject's omnipotent control. . . . (p. 89)

To learn from others is to acquire new thoughts that are not within one's own omnipotent control. There is a group of persons, who as a consequence of developmental trauma, or developmental impingement, need to maintain a system of thought that is entirely within their own omnipotent control. To admit the entry of thoughts from others is to risk the sur-render of this omnipotent control. Hence, such persons cannot learn from experience. This developmental stage, as Winnicott describes in his seminal paper on the transitional object, is linked to the capacity for illusion. The capacity for illusion requires that the subject's inner world enter into the object; this is the basis of all creativity. Learning from the therapeutic en-counter, whether psychotherapy or psychoanalysis, requires this capacity for a *symbolic* transformation of the therapeutic experience. As I have emphasized earlier, it is in this sense that the therapeutic relationship symbolizes early developmental conflict. Without this capacity for symbolic transformation one cannot learn from the therapeutic encounter.

Perhaps due to the narcissism brought about by small or not so small differences, I wish to close my presentation with a comparison of object relations theory to Kohut's (1977) self psychology. For despite Kohut's emphasis upon the *self* as an entity, self psychology is a branch of object relations theory. In a certain sense Kohut's contribution could be viewed as an extension of Winnicott's work. For example, Kohut's introduction of the term *self-object* to describe certain transference manifestations where there is imperfect differentiation between the self and the object may cover some of the same ground as Winnicott's transitional object. There are further similarities such as the emphasis upon trauma and developmental arrest which Kohut prefers to call deficits. However there are also major and significant differences. I speak now for myself; for there is of course no "official" position of object relations theory concerning self psychology. I believe that self psychology is fundamentally a two-person psychology, but this fact has been obscured by Kohut's insistence that the self and not the *self and its object* occupy the center. More significantly object relations theory views the relation between the self and its objects to be intensely conflictual and inseparable from a psychology of guilt (Treurniet, 1980; Wallerstein, 1983; Modell, 1984). This is in contrast to Kohut's view that self psychology is a psychology of deficiency states in contrast to the psychology of conflict intrinsic to classical psychoanalysis. The developmental stage of individuation to which self psychology is addressed is intrinsically conflictual and guilt producing. Kohut has correctly emphasized that the fear of the annihilation or fragmentation of the self is the leading anxiety in narcissistic cases. But this anxiety is embedded in poignant conflict situations. For example, at a fundamental level there is a conflict that may be described as the wish to remain autonomous, self-sufficient, and hidden, versus the wish to surrender, to be found, to be taken over. Due to the waning influence of the Oedipus complex in some narcissistic cases Kohut may have mistakenly assumed that guilt is also less prominent. It appears to me that Kohut has understood only two alternatives: that of the classical Freudian concept of the superego as the heir to the Oedipus complex, or a new psychology of the self in which the Oedipus complex and the superego have little place. Whether or not the Oedipus complex has been displaced in narcissistic cases is a complex issue currently under debate (see appendix), but there is no evidence to suggest that guilt is less frequent in these patients. In addition to the more traditionally understood sources of guilt whose content derives from the Oedipus complex, I have described other forms of guilt derived from the process of individuation itself (1965, 1971). There is a form of guilt that accompanies the process of individuation. There is a widespread, fundamental belief, perhaps a primal fantasy, that separation damages the "other." Similarly, there is a widespread conviction that if one has more of the available "good" others in the nuclear family will be deprived. Becoming autonomous and having a separate life and separate fate from other family members is in itself guilt inducing. A psychology that focuses on the process of individuation must also acknowledge the guilt that accompanies individuation.

Kohut (1982) would see psychosexual conflict and the conflicts associated with the Oedipus complex as avoidable if there were phase appropriate, empathic interactions between parent and child. I do not believe that this is true. I believe Oedipal conflict to be inevitable despite the best of parent–child interactions.

There are then at least four broad groups of object relations theories within contemporary psychoanalysis. Each has its own history, traditions, and, unfortunately, separate languages. What I have presented is basically an object relations theory in the tradition of Balint and Winnicott modified through my own clinical perceptions. Kohut's self psychology is yet another, somewhat overlapping theory, whilst the Kleinian–Bion theory of object relations is a third, again partially overlapping but separate tradition. Kernberg's theory of object relations is another amalgam derived in part from Klein and Fairbairn but placed into the context of ego psychology. It may not be too much to hope that we are now ready to begin the task that will be completed by future generations; that is, to step outside our respective traditions, to find areas of common agreement and understanding that have been masked by the idiosyncratic language and concepts of a particular "school." This is not to minimize the very real conceptual differences that divide us, but we cannot hope to address these issues until we find some common language.

Chapter 7

Lacanian Theory

William J. Richardson, Ph.D.

> One man knelt, cried for a minute and left behind his campaign medals, Purple Heart, Bronze Star, Legion of Merit. Another, like many of the veterans, in olive drab, added his name to an ad hoc battalion sheet someone had staked in the ground; he stood back, saluted, saw his reflection in the black stone, then let out a kind of agonized whimper before two buddies led him away. . . . They came like pilgrims, bigger crowds each day, to Washington's newest and most unorthodox monument: the Viet Nam Veterans Memorial (*Time,* 11/22/82, p. 44).

You recognize this scene: the Washington Mall, November 1982. We all experienced the event, I presume, at least with the help of the media. And we all remember the war—at least since it ended in 1975, and some of us remember it ever since the first U.S. involvement in 1959. It festered in the national conscience as a mélange of grief, guilt, bitterness, and shame. Yet with the unveiling of the monument there was a reconciliation—"a homecoming, at last," one headline said. This took place not just through the paroxysm of emotion (e.g., the weeping, the fingering and kissing of names), but above all by the names themselves of the dead and missing (59,939 of them), listed one by one in the stone—each name uttered again by a living voice through the public reading of them in the National Cathedral. It was as if these men had wandered about like ancient Greek warriors, unburied, but the *naming* of them gave them a place of rest with honor at last, an honor shared with those who survive. It was this naming that was salutary, and in the words of the chief organizer of the tribute, this naming "exposes and thereby ends the denial that has characterized the country's reaction to the war. It is probably the most important step in the process of healing and redemption" (*Time*, 11/22/82, p. 46).

I would like to suggest that the individual therapeutic process, too, is analogous to this event—essentially a naming of the unburied ghosts that haunt us, an identifying of them and fixing them with a name that enables us to put them to rest once and for all. Be that as it may, this event offers us a first paradigm by which to understand the basic orientation of Jacques Lacan as he undertakes the rereading of Freud. For he has introduced a triple distinction that he claims to find unannounced explicitly in Freud, involving the real, the imaginary, and the symbolic. In the example I have mentioned, the real would be the unspeakable dimension of the trauma triggered by the war itself and its aftermath in the common conscience; the imaginary would be, I think, the sensible, visual, physical aspects of the scene, such as the mirror reflections in the marble, the jumble of emotions, and so on; the symbolic is suggested by the naming. All that needs explanation, of course, but let me start with it as a concrete way of trying to understand what in general Lacan is about, so that we can then examine in more detail how he conceives the therapeutic process as such.

It will be easiest to begin, I think, with what Lacan means by the symbolic. But first, a preamble: Essentially, Lacan argues that Freud's epoch-making discovery of the nature of the "talking cure" was an insight into the manner in which language works, but that the only paradigm he had available to make it scientifically respectable was that of nineteenth century physics. Now, another scientific model is available to us—a specifically human one—namely, the science of language, linguistics. Hence, the fundamental proposition of psychoanalysis becomes: "the unconscious (discovered by Freud) is structured in the most radical way like a language" (Lacan, 1977, p. 234).

It was Lévi-Strauss who helped Lacan to see this. His cultural anthropology was based on the analysis of what is most specifically characteristic of human culture: our capacity to symbolize; that is, to re-present the real, to "signify" (*signum facere*), to render present through signs that which is absent. He tries, then, to discern regularities in the ways human beings exercise this symbolic function (e.g., in laws of exchange, kinship relations, myth making, etc.), striving to formulate these regularities in abstract, increasingly universal, algebraic symbols. The ideal is to achieve a kind of periodic table of human regulations, governed by some single, ultimate, and eventually formulable law of symbolic functioning. What is new here is not so much Lévi-Strauss's ambition but his method, for the exercise of the symbolic function par excellence is human language, and he finds both the inspiration and the model for his enterprise in the work of contemporary (so-called "structuralist") linguistics.

Lacan's approach is more properly psychoanalytic than that of Lévi-Strauss, but like the latter he takes as his paradigm the work of structural linguistics, as fathered by Ferdinand de Saussure. Lacan accepts the distinction between language (as system) and speech (as act), where the system is one of signs and, indeed, "closed" upon itself. That means (and this is important for the structuralists) that each element of the system is distinguished only by its opposition to other elements in the same system, like words in a dictionary. Lacan also accepts the distinction in every speech sign between a signifying component ("signifier") and a signified component ("signified"), the former being the speech sound and the latter the mental image (e.g., the sound(s) "Wash-ing-ton" versus the mental image of the place where a particular event took place). Finally, Lacan accepts the arbitrary nature of the relationship between signifier and signified (e.g., "Washington" can refer equally well to the place, to our first president, to a center of government, to the mayor of Chicago).

From de Saussure's disciples (e.g., R. Jakobson) Lacan accepts the thesis that all signifiers are related to each other according to a double axis: one, an axis of "combination," where they follow one another like words in a sentence; the other an axis of "selection," where one signifier excludes another but remains related to it, at least negatively (e.g., calling the event at the war memorial in Washington a "homecoming" excludes calling it a "reunion" or a "celebration"). The axis of combination makes possible what rhetoricians call "metonymy" (e.g., to speak of "Vietnam veterans" is to designate them by contiguity with the place where they served); the axis of selection makes possible what rhetoricians call "metaphor" (e.g., to speak of this event as a "homecoming at last" is to use one very resonant signifier in place of something much more pedestrian (like "dedication ceremony"). This sounds somewhat pedantic, I know, but Lacan capitalizes on it to find the same axes operating in Freud's analysis of dream work in the unconscious. But where Freud speaks of "displacement," Lacan sees the structure of metonymy (which eventually becomes the basis of all free association); where Freud speaks of "condensation" (e.g., "Irma" represents more than one woman in Freud's life), Lacan sees the structure of metaphor. I shall return to all this in a moment, but for now let it suffice to suggest how Lacan understands the "laws of language" that permit him to say that "the unconscious is structured in the most radical way like a language."

But as such these laws do not yet constitute what Lacan, after Lévi-Strauss, calls the "symbolic order," the entire register of symbolic functioning in all of its complexity, for these laws are not simply abstract forms. They are concretized in a "treasurehouse" of signifiers that coalesce for every individual out of a long history. Every child is heir to the myths and legends of the race, the sedimentation of his native language, his ethnic background, ancestral heritage, social milieu, and immediate family context up until the subject that these things structure comes into the world and begins to take over a life. You get the sense of it here:

For 56 hours they read the names in the Gothic confines of the National Cathedral. Rhythmic Spanish names. Tongue-twisting Polish names, guttural German, exotic African, homely Anglo-Saxon names. Chinese, Polynesian, Indian and Russian names. They are names which reach deep into the heart of America, each testimony to a family's decision, sometime in the past, to wrench itself from home and culture to test our country's promise of new opportunities and a better life. They are names drawn from the farthest corners of the world and then, in this generation, sent to another distant corner in a war America has done its best to forget (*Newsweek,* 11/22/82, p. 82).

For the moment, let this suggest only that each name represents an individual subject born into a tradition that preceded him and enmeshed him in a chain of signifiers from the moment he began to be. Add to this each one's personal story, all the forotten memories, repressed impulses, hidden traumata that go into every human life.

The symbolic order for Lacan, then, is this matrix of relationships that functions like the laws of language operating through such a storehouse of signifiers. It is the place where truth appears. Furthermore, this system, so conceived, is a firm and constant principle that Lacan calls "law"—eventually *the* law, the "Law of *the* Father," where the father is thought of not as the physical, living father who actually generated the subject but as the dead father in Freud's myth of origins (in *Totem and Taboo*); that is, the symbolic father, or simply the name-of-the-father, source of all law.

In any case, this circuit is "other" than what the individual is conscious of, hence it is unconscious in its functioning; it is *the* unconscious (Lacan claims) that Freud discovered, and he calls it simply the "Other."

Let that suffice as a brief sketch of what Lacan means by the symbolic order. A word now about the two other registers in the Lacanian epistemology: the register of the imaginary and the register of the real. The imaginary is complementary to the symbolic, and may be said in a general way to be the domain of images, of the sensible representations (more often than not, the visual) that mark all our experience. But Lacan's use of the word is quite special, and to understand it properly we should recall how for him the experience of images begins, namely with the infant's first experience of his ego. Lacan finds warrant for his conception of the ego in Freud's essay "On Narcissism" (1914). There, the ego, instead of being considered an agency or substructure of the personality (of whatever kind), is considered a love object.

The vagaries of the notion of "ego" in Freud's later texts are well known, especially those after 1920, that gave warrant to the ego-psychologists to develop the notion of the ego as mediator between id, superego, and reality—agent of synthesis for the entire personality. For Lacan, however, the 1914 notion of the ego as love object is decisive. Basing his case on data taken from observation in child psychology and animal ethology, Lacan argues that sometime between the ages of six and eighteen months the infant, fragmented by the turmoil of its anarchic urges, perceives, "with a flutter of jubilation" a reflection of itself, whether in a counterpart or in a mirror, as a form (*Gestalt*) by which it anticipates a bodily unity still to be achieved in fact, and with which it identifies. This reflected, therefore alienated image becomes the ideal of eventual unity, the basis for all subsequent identification, and its citadel of defense (1977, pp. 1–7). So the infant, caught up in identification with its mirror image, is locked into a bipolar image-world; that is, in the register of what Lacan calls the imaginary.

The ego, then, is not the subject but alienated image of the subject, or more precisely, of the subject-to-be. How does the subject emerge in the young organism? We have some idea of this from the way Lacan interprets the famous anecdote of Freud's grandchild who, with the o-o-o-o and *da* of the *fort-da* ("away"–"here") experience of making a toy reel disappear and return, plays the game of thereby making his mother disappear and return (Freud, 1920, pp. 14–15). What is striking in this for Lacan is not the fact that by this game of substituting a toy reel for his mother the child learns to control his libidinal urges, but rather that through the exercise of these primitive phonemes the child discovers the marvelous secret that what is absent can be rendered present through signifiers, for he thereby enters into the symbolic order.

But the essential in all this is to see in the experience of the ego as mirror image the model of the imaginary as such; that is, an immediate reciprocity between seer and seen, a dualistic relationship that is unmediated by the distance that language provides. Moreover, the notion of *imago* as mirror image suggests not only a visual but also a spatial and even corporal character in this experience. The result is that for Lacan, every experience of the body or any aspect of it belongs to the register of the imaginary. Finally, the imaginary is the realm of all fantasy, all imaged representations, even representations of words (when the time comes). In the scene at the Washington Mall, the reflected images in the polished black stone are the perfect model of the imaginary, but so, too, is the turmoil of emotion, the weeping, the fingering, and kissing of the names, even the carved granite as such. It is not the physical carving in granite that gives them their symbolic valence but the registration of them in the symbolic order as such.

The third member of Lacan's epistemological triad he calls the "real." Now the real is not "reality" as we usually understand it, the world of ordinary experience—lecture halls, chairs, microphones, and war monuments—for this world is already organized through images and the symbolic structures of language. We can already talk about it and agree about it in the manner of what we call "consensual validation." The real is precisely not "reality" in that sense, but rather the raw experience of what is, the not yet symbolized or imaged, the "impossible" (i.e., impossible to inscribe in any symbolic system or represent in any form of image). For example, the real would be the pain that one patient described a short time ago as "unspeakable," or the awesomeness of the Holocaust, or the horror aboard

KAL 007 after it had been hit by a Russian missile and spiraled toward its doom. But the real, too, is any form of enigma, even the undiscovered secret of the physical universe that science tries to unveil—like Newton's laws before Newton discovered them. In Washington, November 1982, the real was the common anguish that the participants struggled to articulate.

What, then, really happened with the naming of the names? The real of this national trauma found articulation in the symbolic order; it has been transposed into language and thereby has found an appropriate place in the social discourse. Its truth has appeared. It is by naming that the "symbolic relation intervenes," Lacan tells us, for "naming constitutes a pact by which two subjects agree at the same time to recognize the same object" (1954–1955, p. 202). This is true for the giving of any kind of name, common as well as proper. Later he adds, "as soon as (something) can be named, its presence can be evoked as an original dimension, distinct from reality. Nomination is an evocation of presence and maintains presence in absence" (1954–1955, p. 297). In the case of the Vietnam dead, we are dealing in proper names:

> They are names drawn from the farthest corners of the world and then, in this generation, sent to another distant corner in a war America has done its best to forget. But to hear the names being read, and to see them stretching down long expanses of black granite at the new Vietnam Veterans Memorial, is to remember. The war was about names, each name a special human being who never came home (*Newsweek*, 11/22/82, p. 82).

And the paradox is that the naming of these names is not only a way to remember but a way to forget, for it gives the ghosts that haunt us a place of rest, inscribing them with honor in the symbolic order—at last. So, too, is the process of psychoanalysis: the task is to find the true name for the real that has found expression in the symptom and thus inscribe it appropriately in the symbolic order so that the ghosts that haunt us may be properly remembered and then properly forgotten, buried with honor at last.

Of course, one may wonder whether this terminology that distinguishes between symbolic, imaginary, and real has a right to claim Freud for a patron. Clearly, it is Lacan's innovation, but just as clearly it is proposed under the name of a "return to Freud." The matter deserves a study of its own, and it cannot be our purpose to examine it in depth here. Let it suffice to suggest that, just as it is in the early Freud, according to Lacan, that we find the most untrammeled effort to articulate his basic insight, so it is there, too, that we should seek grounds for this distinction.

A careful study would begin, then, with an examination of Freud's prepsychoanalytic writings, particularly his study *On Aphasia* (1891) and the *"Project for a Scientific Psychology"* (1895). It would include, too, those letters to Fliess contemporaneous with these works that might be relevant. Thus, for example, in Letter 52 (12/6/1896), shortly after abandoning definitively the abortive "Project," Freud suggests that what in the "Project" is a system of "facilitations" (*Bahnungen* [i.e., "pathways," "traces"]), may be thought of as a series of tran*script*ions (*Niederschriften*) separating perception from consciousness. "Tran*script*ion," however, suggests writing, hence the order of language. Accordingly, one level of transcription is called "unconscious" (arranged according to perhaps causal relations), another called "preconscious" (attached to "word-presentations" accompanied by certain "hallucinatory activation") (1891, pp. 233–235). The term *word-presentation,* however, suggests the order of speech as distinct from language. The implications of this can only be appreciated by finding one's way through the intricacies of the *Project,* particularly as Freud hypothesizes the genesis of speech out of the infant's scream (1895, pp. 366–367, 373–374). Forrester (1980) summarizes this development as part of his analysis of the role of language in the origins of psychoanalysis.

One can find clearer warrant for this distinction in the

Interpretation of Dreams (1900). In terms of metapsychology, one could show how the reflection of Chapter VII complements the speculation of the "Project," but it is simpler, perhaps, to recall first Freud's note in the analysis of the Irma dream: "There is at least one spot in every dream at which it is unplumable—a navel, as it were, that is its point of contact with the unknown" (1900, p. 111, note 1; cp. p. 525). This dimension that stretches beyond the expressible, or at least beyond the expressed (hence beyond the "known"/"knowable"), is what we understand Lacan to mean by the real. But what of the symbolic and the imaginary? Perhaps the most pertinent formulation in this regard is the following:

> Suppose I have a picture puzzle, a rebus, in front of me. It depicts a house with a boat on its roof, a single letter of the alphabet, the figure of a running man whose head has been conjured away, and so on. Now I might be misled into raising objections and declaring that the picture as a whole and its component parts are nonsensical. A boat has no business to be on the roof of a house; and if the whole picture is intended to represent a landscape, letters of the alphabet are out of place in it since such objects do not occur in nature. But obviously we can only form a proper judgment of the rebus if we put aside criticisms such as these of the whole composition and its parts and if, instead, we try to replace each separate element by a syllable or word that can be represented by that element in some way or other. The words which are put together in this way are no longer nonsensical but may form a poetical phrase of the greatest beauty and significance. A dream is a picture-puzzle of this sort, and our predecessors in the field of dream-interpretation have made the mistake of treating the rebus as a pictorial composition: and as such it has seemed to them nonsensical and worthless. (Freud, 1900, pp. 277–278)

Clearly, the "pictorial composition" here is of the order of images, and hence pertains to what Lacan calls the imaginary. The symbolic functions insofar as "each separate element" is replaced by a syllable or a word "that can be represented by that element" in some way or other. It is precisely this translation of the images into *linguistic* terms (hence, into the order of the symbolic) that differentiates Freud from his predecessors.

But all of this is in the order of theory. Far more illuminating is the example of Freud in action. Let us watch him, then, in full flight as he reports to us the treatment of the famous Dora. Why this old chestnut? (1) In the first place, it is a typically Lacanian move, for he pretends to be doing nothing more than leading his readers back to the text of Freud himself—Freud in action, for him, remains the ultimate paradigm of analytic practice. (2) The Dora case is contemporaneous with the great creative burst that culminated in the *Interpretation of Dreams* (1900–1901)—though published four years later (1905). Here we find the genius of Freud trying to articulate his discovery in its purest form, brilliant even in its failure. (3) All the available data are familiar to everyone without the distraction of novelty. (4) Finally, there is no problem of confidentiality.

The parameters are familiar, of course. Presenting symptoms: breathing difficulty (dyspnoea), nervous cough, speechlessness (aphonia), and possibly migraine, together with depression, hysterical unsociability, and *taedium vitae* (1905, p. 22)—a classic picture of *petite hysterie*. Precipitating event: the indiscreet proposition of Herr K. by the lakeside. Background: Dora's father's ongoing affair with Frau K.; Dora's ambiguous relation to Herr K., her friendliness with Frau K., and special concern for their two children. The thesis I am trying to demonstrate is that the unconscious is structured like a language; that is, the symbolic order (register of the symbolic function) follows certain laws (e.g., of combination and selection) that are fundamentally laws of language. Let us first see how this functions with regard to symptom formation.

Recall how the nervous cough disappeared, for example; Dora was complaining that Frau K. was interested in her father because he was a *Vermögender Mann* ("man of means"), but Freud's theory about the inversion of signifiers permitted him to hear that as an *Unvermögender Mann* ("man without means"), that is, impotent. But if that were so how could there be a normal love affair between them? Dora acknowledges that there can be more than one form of sexual gratification. With this much to work with, Freud moves quickly to see the spasmodic cough as a substitute for the meaning or presumed *fellatio* between the two lovers. The structure is one of metaphor, then, and the symptom disappears when the substitution is articulated in words (1905, pp. 47–48), that is, when the appropriate name is found.

Again, take Dora's speechlessness (aphonia). She reports that Frau K. falls ill when Herr K. returns from a trip and regains her health when he leaves again. When Dora alludes to an alternation between good and bad health in childhood, Freud seizes the opportunity to ask about the periodicity of her present symptom. In point of fact, the speechlessness begins when Herr K. is away, disappears when he returns, and in the meantime her writing skills improve proportionately, for the two correspond. "When the man she loved was away," Freud tells us, "she gave up speaking; speech had lost its value since she could not speak to *him*. On the other hand, writing gained in importance, as being the only means of communication with him in his absence" (1905, p. 40). In short, her speechlessness, as symptom, is a substitute for, therefore expression of, her unconscious love for Herr K.—it is a metaphor (i.e., a structure of language).

None of this is terribly problematic, for all we are adding to familiar data is an insistence on the linguistic model of metaphor. More interesting, perhaps, is the function of metonymy as this appears in Freud's analysis of the first of Dora's dreams. You will recall the text:

> A house was on fire. My father was standing beside my bed and woke me up. I dressed quickly. Mother wanted to stop and save her jewel-case; but Father said: "I refuse

to let myself and my two children be burnt for the sake of your jewel-case." We hurried downstairs, and as soon as I was outside I woke up (1905, p. 64).

Dora's first association is to her father's objection to the mother's wish that her brother be locked in his room, for "something might happen in the night so that it might be necessary to leave the room" (1905, p. 65). Freud calls attention to the exact words she uses, repeats them back to her, since they "may have to return to them," then adds in a footnote:

> I laid stress on these words because they took me aback. They seemed to have an ambiguous ring about them. Are not certain physical needs referred to in the same words? Now, in a line of associations ambiguous words (or, as we may call them, "switch words") act like points at a junction. If the points are switched across from the position in which they appear to lie in the dream, then we find ourselves on another set of rails; and along this second track run the thoughts which we are in search of but which still lie concealed behind the dream (1905, p. 65 no. 1).

We can't follow the analysis in detail, of course, but let me recall two themes: (1) the jewel case; (2) the fire. "What's this about the jewel-case your mother wants to save?" says Freud. Jewelry suggests the pearl drops her mother wanted but instead her father gave her mother a bracelet that she rejected. Dora would have liked to receive such a gift from her father. But the jewel case? Herr K. had given her the present of a jewel case. Freud: "then a return present would have been very appropriate. Perhaps you do not know that 'jewel-case' (*Schmuckkästchen*) is a favourite expression . . . for female genitals" (1905, p. 69). Here Freud goes beyond the patient's conscious intention to find a meaning in the sedimentation of language itself as found in the treasury of the signifiers that constitutes the symbolic order. Freud makes a similar move with regard to the locking/not-locking of the room, for he adds in a note:

> I suspected, though I did not as yet say so to Dora, that

she had seized upon this element on account of a symbolic meaning which it possessed. *"Zimmer"* ("room") in dreams stands very frequently for *"Frauenzimmer"* (a slightly derogatory word for "woman"; literally "woman's apartments"). The question whether a woman is "open" or "shut" can naturally not be a matter of indifference. It is well known, too, what sort of "key" effects the opening in such a case (1905, p. 67, note 1).

How does Dora's mother enter the dream?

She is, as you know, your former rival for your father's affections. In the incident of the bracelet, you would have been glad to accept what your mother had rejected. Now let us just put "give" instead of "accept" and "withhold" instead of "reject." Then it means that you were ready to give your father what your mother withheld from him, and the thing in question was connected with jewelry (1905, p. 70).

Notice how Freud makes his interpretive move by a purely linguistic reversal ("give" instead of "accept," "withhold" in place of "reject"). It is the function of verbal antithesis, then, that permits Freud to use this familiar tactic, and enables him to hear a signifier articulated through its opposite (e.g., the "man of means" as "man without means").

This is exactly what happens in the analysis of the fire theme. For by the function of antithesis, fire suggests its opposite, water, and the notion of water (wetness) leads Freud a long way. For example:

I notice that the antithesis of water and fire has been extremely useful to you in the dream. Your mother wanted to save the jewel-case so that it should not be *burnt,* while in the dream-thoughts it is a question of the "jewel-case" not being *wetted.* But fire is not only used as the contrary of water, it also serves directly to represent love (as in the phrase "to be *consumed* with love"). So that from "fire" one set of rails runs by way of this symbolic meaning to thoughts of love; while the other set runs by way of the contrary "water," and, after sending off a branch line which provides another connection with "love" (for love also makes things wet), leads in a different direction. And what direction can that be? (1905, p. 72)

The direction of bed-wetting, of course, and with it the memory of Dora's father waking her at night (as in the dream) to help prevent it; then eventually the role of masturbation in the genesis of her neurosis. For our purposes, it suffices to see that the entire analysis here turns on a consideration of a signifier (fire) as a "switch-word," hence upon a purely linguistic operation.

Freud puts it all together in his synthesis of the dream, in which his interpretation is essentially based on the concatenation of signifiers that is supported, like a vine on a trellis, by the structure of language itself. He sees the word *wet* as a nodal point between several group of ideas. The first series includes: bed-wetting, wetness in sexual intercourse, the wetness presented to a woman in the form of drops. A second series suggests dirtiness: the vaginal catarrh ("Switchword," 1905, p. 82), a sign of being dirtied, the mother dirtied by the father's seminal drops as also by the disease she contracted from him: "gonorrhea." These two series cross each other in the word *drops*—another "switchword" (1905, p. 90)—which is correlated with "jewelry" (recall the pearl drops the mother wanted) as well as with seminal discharge. But it was not her jewelry but her jewel case that mother wanted to save. "Case" here introduces the series of words related to Herr K., his seduction and his "gift." Recapitulating, Freud says:

The composite word thus formed, "jewel-case," had beyond this a special claim to be used as a representative element in the dream. Is not "jewel-case" a term commonly used to describe female genitals that are immaculate and intact? And is it not, on the other hand, an innocent word? Is it not, in short, admirably calculated both to betray and

to conceal the sexual thoughts that lie behind the dream? . . .
The element of "jewel-case" was more than any other a
product of condensation and displacement, and a compromise between contrary mental currents (1905, pp.
91–92).

In all this it is essential to see that the fantasies of the
imaginary are transposed, through the analysis of words and
the articulation of that analysis, into the symbolic. It is not a
matter of reducing the experience to "words and nothing else"
(vox et praeterea nihil); rather, through the power of language
(i.e., the symbolic function) things become present in their absence; that is, they are given a *name,* and the truth of the matter
is able slowly to appear.

If we bring the matter up to date in terms of the discussion
that serves as the theme for this volume, it is striking that Jacob
Arlow, in presenting the classical Freudian model of the mind,
lauds the structural theory as "the best model, the most effective
and comprehensive theory by which one can conceptualize the
phenomenology of mental conflict" (p. 22), but then, in order
to explain it, transposes the theory into a linguistic mode. "Free
associations [orally articulated, no doubt] offer a living record
of the moment to moment functioning of the patient's mind"
(p. 22). This function is seen as a conversation within the patient
to which the psychoanalyst is "privy," a conversation that includes many voices, each of which, with the analyst's help, must
be heard. And as in any conversation, "context" is everything—comprehension derives not just from the content but
from "sequence" and "juxtaposition" ("contiguity") in the flow
of what is articulated. In other words, the entire discourse is
governed by the principle of metonymy.

Thus, in the case of the deformed young man who fantasized blowing up the city of New York (analyst included), it
is the *context* of his question about confidentiality that supplied
its meaning and permitted the underlying conflict to be articulated, as Arlow hypothesizes, in the following fashion: " 'I'd
like to kill everyone in the city, even my analyst. But that's not

right. He's trying to help. It's a terrible thought. I'm ashamed of it. I don't like myself for thinking such thoughts. What would people think if they found out? I hope they never do' " (p. 32). In Lacanian terms here, the inarticulate conflict would be the locus of the real, the fantasy with its affective valence, a function of the imaginary, and the verbal articulation of the "full text, if we could restore it," the function of the symbolic. Thus, the elements of the discourse are somehow related, "very much in the way that one word following another gives meaning to a sentence and one sentence following another gives meaning to a paragraph" (p. 23).

Arlow calls this manner of conceiving the structural theory a "quasi-parable" (p. 24), which illustrates "the principle that the structures of the mind, as organized around the concept of the role each one plays in intrapsychic conflict, do indeed reflect and specify some aspect of the functioning of the psyche of a person, the analysand" (p. 24). Fair enough! But one may then ask if the justification for the quasi-parable may not be that underneath the structural theory and making it possible is the fact that the laws of language itself govern the psychoanalytic interchange. At any rate, this is how a Lacanian would see the matter.

Chapter 8

A Discussion of the Various Theories

Joseph Sandler, Ph.D., M.D.

I will start with a consideration of the relation of theory to clinical work by presenting some clinical material of my own. Following an excellent but very substantial dinner, coupled with the effects of jet lag, I awoke very early this morning with an anxiety dream. The content of the dream was simply that I was being given an oral examination in German. My associations took me to a paper soon to be presented in Vienna, which I have to deliver in German, a language in which I am far from fluent. I was aware that I had been worrying about this for some time, but then the meaning of the dream occurred to me. It seemed clear that by displacing my anxiety from this discussion to the Vienna paper I was effectively postponing today's presentation. My satisfaction with this piece of analytic work allowed me to doze off again, but I woke soon with sudden recall of a memory of something that had occurred a very long time ago. In order to qualify for my Master's degree I had to pass an examination in scientific German. I was quite confident that I could do this on the basis of my very scanty knowledge, and went into the examination room, with some half-a-dozen others, to find that we had each been given a copy of Grimm's fairy tales in German, and were told to translate the story of Hansel and Gretel with the aid of a German dictionary. I didn't do it very well and was rather nervous about this. The examiner gathered up the papers at the end of the hour, put them in his pocket, walked to the door, paused for a moment and said, "You've all passed." I realized then that what I wanted to say this morning to the contributors was this: "You've all passed," and this again enabled me to doze off. But I couldn't fall asleep readily, and after an internal struggle realized that what I really wanted to say was that their clinical work was terrible and they had all failed. Of course I could not say such a thing about the various presentations. It would be completely unacceptable to tell Dr. Arlow, for example, that he had failed to take up his patient's transference concern about the analyst's health, to tell Dr. Segal that she hadn't distinguished between the patient's fantasies and her own, and to suggest that anyone bringing a Kleinian paper to New York, famous as a stronghold of ego-psychology, would have to feel persecuted by a thousand little computers. How could I say to Dr. Levenson that he provided his patient with chances to use intellectualization as a defense against the transference? How could I conceivably comment to Dr. Goldberg that he should have analyzed his patient's bitter resentment and aggression in the transference, that conflict can be preoedipal, and that his patient was full of such conflicts that should have been interpreted? It would certainly be improper to say to Dr. Modell that the problems his patient described related more to failures in his internal object relationships rather than his external ones, that the analyst should have focused more specifically on the analysis of resistance in the transference.

Chapters 2 through 7 illustrate how six different psychoanalytic cultures reflect not only different theoretical models, but also different sets of values. Anthropologists have described for us just how difficult it is to reach the understanding that the anthropologist himself possesses a culture, just as much as do the people he is studying. Analysts in a way have a similar problem. It is very difficult to accept fully that all sorts of historical, developmental, and personal factors have entered into our own theories and styles of clinical practice. It is very tempting to assume that those who work as we do are good analysts, and those who do not are bad. And in spite of what we may say in polite society, I think that secretly we all believe our own system to be right, and the systems of others, to the extent that they differ from our own, to be wrong or to reflect inadequate insight or training. Charles Brenner has commented that we cannot say that all theories are equal, and I agree with him entirely. But it is not, of course, a question of which theory is right and which wrong, but rather to what extent a theory is good theory. Obviously we have to accept that all the theoretical models that have been presented are to some degree good and useful, and here I would endorse what Arnold Cooper has emphasized in his paper; that our models must relate to what the analyst actually does, and the more this can be shown and discussed, the better our theories will be. For this reason a book of this sort is particularly rewarding.

The issue of the relation of clinical work to our models of the mind is not straightforward. We do not simply invent or adopt a theory and apply it to our clinical work. In this regard I would like to advocate the adoption of a historical-developmental view of psychoanalytic theory, much as Dr. Cooper has done. Psychoanalytic theory has, throughout its life, been in a state of continuous though uneven development, and as ideas have progressed on one front, so there have been repercussions in other areas, leading to states of conceptual strain of one sort or another. It is a very good thing that this happens, that we do not have a complete and closed theory, because it is the very existence of these states of theoretical strain which continually occur as our theory lurches forward in this direction or that, that provides a major dynamic for conceptual development. Every new definition and every new gain in precision puts pressure on other aspects of theory. In particular, concepts become stretched to encompass new ideas and new insights, with a resulting shift of meaning in our concepts. For example, the notion of fantasy first referred to daydreams, and then the term was extended to include unconscious fantasy. But unconscious fantasy encompasses preconscious fantasy, which is descriptively unconscious in the topographical sense (belonging to the unconscious ego in terms of the structural theory) as well as fantasy that has been repressed into the system unconscious (or into the id). With the extension of the concept by Susan Isaacs to cover a much broader spectrum of mental content, it has acquired a very wide range of meanings indeed. The same process of extension holds true for the concept of transference, which was originally seen as the repetition of an aspect of a past relationship in an inappropriate way in the present. Yet as we have come to know more about the way in which defenses involving interpersonal interactions are used in the analytic situation, we have tended to call these interactions transference as well. The concept has become stretched and we could say that a state of strain has developed within it.

If we take a historical-developmental viewpoint we can escape quarrels about which theory is right and which is wrong. We are then in the position of being able to ask why this, that, or the other formulation was put forward. We can ask, as Dr. Cooper has done, what has prompted writers to formulate their particular theories in the way they have. We have to assume, even if we disagree with their clinical approach and theoretical formulation, that each has good and valid reasons for the aspects he has chosen to emphasize. I should like to suggest that the differences between us (and we see the differences much more readily than the common ground) result inevitably from the fact that psychoanalysis is not a complete theory and has not developed in an orderly fashion, with the result that the joints between different aspects of it have of necessity become very elastic.

In a recent paper (Sandler, 1983) I attempted to trace some of the connections between psychoanalytic theory and practice, and commented:

> It is of some interest that whenever an aspect of theory has emphasis transferred from it to some new formulation, so the hiatuses and weak areas in the theory which follow (if

only because the new theory never encompasses exactly the same area as the old) attract counterforces aimed at filling the gaps or remedying the weaknesses. It is characteristic of these counterforces that they inevitably push forward a core of ideas which are useful and important; equally inevitably they represent an over-reaction, an over-filling of the empty spaces. Gaps and weaknesses in theory also follow changes in specific areas resulting from advances in clinical psychoanalysis and in technical procedures; again, sooner or later over-reactions occur. And if the proponent of the new ideas is a charismatic leader, then a new "movement" in psychoanalysis may result. It may split from the mainstream of psychoanalysis, or remain within it, contributing to the dialectic of theoretical development (pp. 35–36).

Dr. Arlow has provided us very well with the necessary stabilizing function of the classical structural model, as well as with a necessary reminder of the importance of conflict. What is shown so well in his chapter, however, is how the theoretical models we use operate at different levels. It is, I suppose, not to be avoided that the presentation of a theory in its application to clinical work must make it appear as if one can in fact fully spell out the real theory behind one's work. I am convinced that this is not the case in psychoanalysis. What happens as one gains experience as a psychoanalyst has been described as follows (Sandler, 1983):

> The fledgling psychoanalyst will bring with him into his consulting room what he has learned from his own analyst, from his supervisors and other teachers and from his reading. He will carry in his head theoretical and clinical propositions that he has gathered from these various sources, and these propositions will be, for the most part, the official, standard or public ones. The human mind being what it is, he will continue to underestimate the discrepancies and incongruities in the public theories and will

learn to move from one part of his theory to another without being aware that he has stepped over a number of spots in his theory that are conceptually weak. With increasing clinical experience the analyst, as he grows more competent, will preconsciously (descriptively speaking unconsciously) construct a whole variety of theoretical segments which relate directly to his clinical work. They are the products of unconscious thinking, are very much partial theories, models or schemata, which have the quality of being available in reserve, so to speak, to be called upon whenever necessary. That they may contradict one another is no problem. They coexist happily as long as they are unconscious. They do not appear in consciousness unless they are consonant with what I have called official or public theories, and can be described in suitable words. Such partial structures may in fact represent better (i.e., more useful and appropriate) theories than the official ones, and it is likely that many valuable additions to psychoanalytic theory have come about because conditions have arisen that have allowed preconscious part-theories to come together and emerge in a plausible and psychoanalytically socially acceptable way (pp. 37–38).

In his paper Dr. Arlow places great emphasis on conflict between the psychic structures. He comments, "to my way of thinking this [the structural] theory remains the best model, the most effective and comprehensive theory by which one may conceptualize the phenomenology of mental conflict." This is a statement of "official" theory. But I have no doubt that Dr. Arlow, in his clinical work, is highly sensitive to conflicts that are not here-and-now derivatives of conflicts between the psychic agencies. I have no doubt either that he has an implicit model of mental functioning which includes the idea of conflict over many things not necessarily directly related to id or superego; for example, "unconscious conflicts of the highest clinical importance relating to fear of being socially disgraced if one behaves in a child-like defensive fashion" (Sandler, 1974).

We can regard the structural theory, in the form in which it was put forward by Freud, as being a reaction to all the accumulating limitations and contradictions of a top-heavy topographical model. Inevitably, this was an overreaction, and for many the structural model has proven increasingly inadequate. As a result we see overreactions to its inadequacy, exemplified, I believe, in some of the theoretical and clinical stances taken in a number of the chapters in this book.

Dr. Segal has presented us with a Kleinian view, and here again I believe that we see a development from a reaction, inevitably an overreaction, emerging in the 1920s, to specific gaps in classical theory. With the structural model, for example, the notion of "depth" tended to be lost and the place of unconscious fantasy was not clear. Kleinian developments can equally be taken to be a reaction, I believe, to the underestimation of the importance of preoedipal experiences in general, and of early object relationships in particular.

Again, I believe we can see in Dr. Levenson's presentation of a Sullivanian point of view how a theory has developed as a reaction to something missing in our psychoanalytic thinking in regard to interpersonal interaction, and again, inevitably, the part has taken over from the whole, and expanded into a complete system. In all of this the nucleus of appropriateness is important, because Sullivan addressed himself, as did other "deviationists" to an area which indeed required attention, and we should take that seriously, and not throw the baby out with the bathwater. Similarly Dr. Goldberg has shown us Kohut's need to emphasize neglected preoedipal factors, especially the deficits that enter into character formation, which were understressed in the past. One of the reasons, I believe, for Kohut's initial popularity was the relative rigidity of "official" psychoanalytic technique, leading to a situation in which a large discrepancy existed between the public theory on the one hand and implicit theories on the other. Kohut's formulations acted as a license for implicit theory and practice to become explicit, and for the analyst to accept that he could relate to certain patients in ways that he had previously felt were not "official." A similar phenomenon could be seen when Eissler (1953) first introduced the notion of parameters. The concept became extremely popular because one could depart from standard practice if necessary, as long as one came back to it before the end of the analysis. However, the nucleus of appropriateness in Kohut's theory has spread into the whole of his model of the mind. This is probably an unavoidable development, one that in its turn must evoke counterreactions to remedy this system's faults and weaknesses. I have the impression that Dr. Goldberg's paper reflects something of this.

Dr. Modell's presentation again, demonstrates a reaction to the relative neglect of object relationships in a basically drive-oriented psychoanalysis, and he has focused on the important role of the object in early development. So we get the emphasis on Winnicott and Fairbairn, and object relations theory in general. And we can be grateful too, to Dr. Richardson for helping us toward an understanding of Lacan's work, because obscure as much of it is, it fills a gap in our psychoanalytic thinking about the structure and organization of what is unconscious. I found Dr. Richardson's paper useful in forging a link between the use of language and the actualization of the feeling of the presence of the introjects, which is important for our psychic survival. Although Lacan's contribution, like Kohut's, has "peaked" after its initial popularity, it is its legacy that will be important for psychoanalysis.

As psychoanalysts each of us makes use of different frameworks and different models, within the context of a general theoretical schema that is not well articulated. But this doesn't mean that we can use lots of models and theories to make a sort of Irish stew of them, and arrive at a composite, an amalgam. In the context of psychoanalytic clinical work, eclecticism is not to be desired. What *is* needed, however, is continual clarification of psychoanalytic theory. In particular I would like to urge the development of psychoanalytic research that attempts to get into the open the *intrinsic* models that analysts actually use in their work. I am convinced that the results of such investigations can be of the greatest value for psychoanalysis.

It would be useful if a way could be found to follow up the discussion in this book by considering *one* model of the mind, not six, and to let the six proponents of different points of view suggest how the model might be improved. I can think of a dozen ways in which Kleinian theory, for example, might be made more consistent and acceptable, without doing violence to its essence. Its clinical value is undoubted, but it is perhaps on the theoretical level that many of us have our most major disagreements. This is also true for other models, and I have no doubt that the same operation could be performed on my own theoretical views. But it may be that such a project is too much for us to swallow because we all overvalue our own belief systems and our systems of thought.

Chapter 9

Conclusion

Arnold Rothstein, M.D.

In writing these concluding remarks I am acutely aware that my commitments to the structural hypothesis and to a metatheoretical perspective on its evolutionary development, significantly influence my experience of the alternative theories upon which I am about to comment. In addition, although recognizing heuristic advantages in a hermeneutic perspective, I find myself critical of some of its implications and interested in some version of a positivistic perspective on the development of psychoanalysis. Nevertheless I have been able to "try a theory on," to immerse myself in it in an attempt to experience its usefulness in analytic work. These experiences have convinced me that there is considerable value in thinking about what might be helpful in the ideas of colleagues with whom I have considerable disagreement.

This book has explored the relationships of psychoanalytic theories to clinical work. It is clear that theory is intended to organize clinical data and thereby facilitate an understanding of what is experienced in the therapeutic situation. However, it is equally clear that theory serves a number of more personal functions for the analyst. Analysts employ theories to create the illusion that they have an answer or *the* answer in the therapeutic encounter, an encounter that is intrinsically filled with uncertainty. Theories provide models or puzzle solutions, terms and procedures, all of which, if properly employed, enhance an analyst's self-esteem. In addition, theories are associated with traditions and institutions which further enhance the analyst's self-esteem as he works within them, and provide both illusions of security and tangible benefits such as referrals. This institutionalization of theory has contributed to an emphasis upon, and exaggeration of, differences and has interfered with more optimal communication between proponents of different points of view. As compared to many psychoanalytic institutes, the institution of the American Psychoanalytic Association is more eclectic and explicitly interested in facilitating communication between members with different points of view. In this regard Sandler's notion that there are publicly held theories and evolving, partially unconscious private theories is both interesting and a potential facilitator of self-analysis.

The early development of psychoanalysis was characterized by its emphasis on Freud's creativity. Cooper emphasized that Freud nurtured his own creativity and discouraged dissent. There followed a process of competition between disciples and dissenters. The disciple is by nature more compliant than the dissenter. He has a more reflexive tendency to agree, confirm, and find security within Freud's theories and in identification with him; at best the disciple elaborates. Dissenters are more defiant and may be afflicted with "divine mistrust" (Erikson, 1954). Characterologically, they may have more creative potential than the disciples. They reflexively tend to disagree, ferret out exceptions, and build theories based on those exceptions. In addition, potential creators may feel their own analysis to be incomplete and through postanalytic insight focus on a deemphasized aspect of Freud's theory. Finally, potential innovators may be more sensitive to the limits of their therapeutic work and seek new ways to lessen the frustrations of that experience. In a related vein, innovations have emerged in response to the challenging frustrations of working on the peripheries of the widening scope with schizophrenics (Sullivan) and narcissistic personality disorders (Kohut).

Six models have been presented here, and the inevitable questions that arise are these: What is similar and different in

what these colleagues do, and how do they think about what
they do? What is central to their ideas of pathogenesis and
mode of therapeutic action?

All analysts interpreted; they differed in regard to what
they interpreted, when they interpreted, and what relative importance they gave to interpretation in their conceptions of the
mode of therapeutic action of psychoanalysis.

Arlow emphasized the interpretation of unconscious conflict as the essence of his point of view. He emphasized the
interpretation of unconscious fantasy created as a compromise
formation from the relative contributions of the three, in part,
unconscious mental agencies of the mind. However, he noted
that the centrality of the Oedipus complex in neurogeneses is
not an essential of his model, thereby leaving it open to assimilate the influence of other factors.

Segal, in presenting Klein's theories, emphasized that they
were an elaboration of Freud's structural model, stressing the
preoedipal development of the ego and the superego. Klein has
been criticized for attributing complex fantasies to infants in
the first year of life, for her excessive emphasis on the death
instinct, and the derivative aggressive drive, for her deemphasis
of the role of real parents in development, and for emphasis
on early interpretation of derivatives of hypothesized preoedipal conflict. In regard to the first criticism, although I think
Mahler's conceptions are more complex, if Klein's timetable
were shifted to the second year of life one can see considerable
concordance between Klein's infant's progressive shift from the
paranoid–schizoid position to the depressive position, and Mahler's infant's development toward object constancy. Some quotes
from Mahler et al. (1975) reflect these similarities.

> In some children ... the rapprochement crisis leads to
> great ambivalence and even to splitting of the object world
> into "good" and "bad," the consequences of which may
> later become organized into neurotic symptoms of the nar-
> cissistic variety. In still other children, islands of devel-
> opmental failures might lead to borderline symptomatology
> in latency and adolescence (p. 229).

The tendency toward splitting of the object world, which may ensue as the child's solution to the pain of longings and losses of the rapprochement crisis, must make for greater difficulty in the resolution of the complex object-related conflicts of the oedipal period. . . .

In these, and perhaps in other diverse ways, we believe, the infantile neurosis becomes manifestly visible at the oedipal period; but it may be shaped by the fate of the rapprochement crisis *that precedes it* (p. 230).

Segal acknowledged Klein's deemphasis of the role of the real parent but suggested that Bion's conception of the parent as container of projective identifications and the corollary potential internalization of that container function remedied Klein's excessive emphasis on conflict concerning drives. It is fascinating to note that proponents of older theories have worked to assimilate and evolve in response to an awareness of this deemphasis while more recent theories have been built upon it.

Finally one is left with the realization that very significant differences remain between what and when a Kleinian would interpret and what the other members of the workshop would do in their clinical work. Segal advocates both early and "deep" interpretation of hypothesized derivatives of preoedipal conflicts.

Striking differences between a so-called traditional perspective and an interpersonal point of view were noteworthy both in what Levenson did in his clinical work and how he thought about what he did. He is interested in the complexity of the surface. In his focus upon what is visible he emphasized interaction. His interpretations focus upon what goes on between people and aim to help his patients better understand interactions and better adapt to them. Two striking similarities were noteworthy between Sullivan and Kohut. Sullivan's conception that "fantasy is considered more the reflection of poorly comprehended real-life interpersonal experience than the emergence from the depths of solipsistic, primitive impulse"

(p. 49) is similar to Kohut's conception of certain primitive fantasies associated with perversions or oedipal conflicts as disintegration products of the self. In addition, Sullivan's idea that "Needs *need* not cause anxiety . . . when they do it is essentially an interpersonal process" (p. 54) is similar to Kohut's and Winnicott's emphasis on the importance of the real personality of parents for personality development.

Modell is writing from the perspective of both preoedipal deficit and conflict. He conceives of preoedipal conflicts concerning individuation that are fraught with guilt. He conceives of intrasystemic ego conflict between "the wish to remain autonomous . . . versus the wish to surrender" (p. 98), and conceives of guilt in response to the fantasy that separation damages "the other." Although Modell believes his views are valuable in understanding the larger question of mode of therapeutic action, his emphasis is on the value of his object relations theory for the treatment of deficit particularly as it manifests itself in sicker "narcissistic" patients.

Modell conceived of his patient as lacking a capacity for trust and the derivative ability to learn from another, analogous to a person physically lacking an organ. Modell conceives of analysis as, in part, "a *symbolic* recreation of aspects of early mother–child reaction" (p. 90). This perspective suggests that *"issues concerning autonomy and self/object differentiation are carried forward and worked through symbolically during the entire life cycle"* (p. 90) and may be worked out in the transference. I find difficulty with Modell's view that patients present mistrust entirely because of early preoedipal failures in mothering. Mistrust may be influenced by later experiences and reflect what Mehlman (1976) has referred to as "secondary mistrust" (p. 23). In addition, a patient's wish to be "held" may reflect a regressive wish to escape from fantasized consequences of oedipal conflict. On the other hand Modell's technical recommendations concerning tact and sensitivity at early stages of analytic work can be most helpful.

Goldberg framed his presentation of self psychology in a

hermeneutic metatheoretical perspective that he believes is intrinsic to all scientific activity. There are no theory-free facts;
theories create facts. He believes that theories are different.
One theory cannot be translated into another; rather, they must
be judged on the basis of criteria of "coherence, comprehensiveness, and consistency." Like Modell, Goldberg emphasized
the importance of the analyst's sensitivity to patients' narcissistic
vulnerabilities. He emphasized the importance of interpretation
of the patient's responses to the analyst's inevitable empathic
failures rather than the interpretation of conflict. The mode
of therapeutic action of psychoanalysis is related to that interpretive process. Its relationship to transmuting internalization and repair of developmental deficit was not elaborated on
in this presentation.

Richardson's presentation of Lacan was fascinating in that
I had no sense of the questions of similarity or difference to
Freud or to a more contemporary traditional perspective as
elaborated by Arlow. Rather Richardson presented Lacan as a
complementary rendering of Freud from a linguistic perspective. Richardson suggested that Lacan translated Freud's ep-
ochal discovery that was expressed in the language of nineteenth
century physics into that of twentieth century linguistics. For
example, Lacan employed the terms *metonymy* for condensation
and *metaphor* for displacement in his discussion of the dreamwork. For me, displacement and condensation are not terms of
physics. Rather, they are terms Freud borrowed from physics
and gave new meaning by transposing them into the metaphors
of a new language of a new field. However, Lacan's concepts
of the real, the imaginary, and the symbolic order enlivened
the familiar from a different organizing perspective and lend
fresh if not new meaning to Freud's insights.

In concluding this volume we are left with a number of
questions concerning the future of psychoanalysis. Perhaps the
most important is, What are the means to evaluate the clinical
value of a theory? Cooper emphasized that by clearly defining
a theory and implicitly emphasizing differences between the-

ories, clinical data could better be evaluated by asking questions concerning the clinical efficacies of work influenced by different theoretical perspectives.

In regard to the clinical vignettes presented in this volume, it seems probable that the authors selected data to emphasize the essence of a model. Such an enterprise inevitably emphasizes differences. In the discussion it was suggested that although the presentations clearly demonstrated differences it might be that successful analytic work shared many similarities and that good results were more similar than different in spite of analysts' theoretical differences. Such a perspective is both interesting and challenging. It suggests we have more to learn about the mode of therapeutic action of psychoanalysis.

There is another question related to the development of theory: Could one theory assimilate a previously deemphasized subject that is being emphasized by a new theory, and thereby evolve into a more complex theory, thus obviating the need for the new theory, or is something essential lost in the translation? I would suggest that the former is true: that the structural hypothesis, for example, can and is assimilating a number of areas deemphasized by Freud. Others, most explicitly Goldberg, but also Levenson, emphasize that the essential new insight and new "facts" that are created by the new theoretical perspective are lost in the translation.

Another important question concerned the issue of the value of a particular theory for a limited group of patients. Are Sullivan's, Modell's, and Kohut's perspectives particularly valuable in working with schizophrenics or more "narcissistic" patients, or are they general models?

It is clear from this book that significant disagreement exists and questions remain relating to our understanding of the relationships of preoedipal to Oedipal and postoedipal experience.

Finally, very important questions were raised concerning the psychoanalytic mode of therapeutic action. Some of these questions will undoubtedly be the focus of future volumes in this series.

Appendix

The Spontaneous
Discussion

This chapter is similar to a panel report in that it summarizes the spontaneous discussion that was a central aspect of the workshop. The discussion consisted of statements concerning psychoanalytic theory and its development and more clinically focused statements about the data presented.

All the panelists conceived of their theories as arising in relationship to, out of, and/or in response to Freud's revolutionary and pioneering accomplishments. They differed somewhat in how they conceived of the post-Freudian process of the development of psychoanalytic theory and in their views of the appropriate strategies for the current and future development of psychoanalysis.

The primarily facilitating participants, Drs. Cooper, Rothstein, and Sandler, as well as the panel chairmen all espoused some version of an evolutionary conception of the development of psychoanalytic theory.

Dr. Cooper reiterated his view that Freud was the only truly revolutionary psychoanalyst. In that regard Cooper conceives of subsequent psychoanalytic creators as proposing a model in the narrow sense or a "concrete puzzle solution" to deal with a particular problem. Cooper emphasized that each limited problem-solving hypothesis then expanded into a general theory of the mind hypothesizing a unifactorial "first cause" conception of development, pathogenesis, and mode of therapeutic action. Cooper emphasized his view that each model was limited and, despite the anxiety-evoking nature of that idea, he felt it was fruitful anxiety for the field's mature growth and should be tolerated and accepted.

Sandler's formal discussion emphasized the irrational factors in practicing psychoanalysts' experience of psychoanalytic theories. He reiterated his view that psychoanalysts have public (explicit) and private (implicit) models. Sandler suggested that when people present their theoretical models in public, or even to their conscious selves, they attempt to do so in the most coherent manner that will avoid their appearing "silly" or "stupid." He commented that in private we have an imperfect conglomerate of theories or part theories. For example, when he thinks from a developmental perspective Sandler might, at various times, think in terms of Freud's psychosexual stages, Mahler's stages of the process of separation–individuation, Erikson's stages of the life cycle, and even of Klein's conception of development from the paranoid–schizoid position through the depressive position, without necessarily feeling compelled to integrate these differing perspectives into a unified and precise theory of development. As a further example, Sandler suggested that, in regard to mental conflict, he doubted that practitioners who work from the organizing perspective of the structural theory—and who stoutly maintain it in public and in their conscious thinking—think predominantly in terms of conflict between the major structures, even though they may say and believe that they do. The good clinician for the most part looks for and implicitly thinks in terms of conflict between a wish or impulse that was acceptable to the individual at some time in the past, and an opposing force that arose later. In some way a notion of ego as "self" has to be taken into account, ". . . . but then one has to speak in terms of self-representations rather than self, and that becomes clumsy." Then with facilitating humor Dr. Sandler added, "Strictly speaking, we should say that the ego is sometimes id-ish and at other times superego-ish, but that sort of formulation can also be difficult."

Somewhat later, in the context of discussing clinical material, Dr. Sandler elaborated his view of the relationships of psychoanalytic theory to clinical work. Sandler stated that he saw the aim of psychoanalytic therapy as being to help the patient to be aware of and more comfortable with the infantile aspects of himself—more precisely, with the adult versions of the "child" parts of himself—including the unconscious current versions of past childhood relationships to the various figures in his internal world. Different models of the mind, although they lead to different interpretations, may nevertheless achieve that aim (although always only partially). Some models are undoubtedly better than others for this purpose, but Sandler suggested that it was quite possible that Dr. Jacob Arlow, working from the perspective of the structural hypothesis, and Dr. Edgar Levenson, working from the vantage point of his personal integration of interpersonal theory, might equally achieve the therapeutic aim—all interpretation uses metaphor, and we should ask not whether one set of metaphors is right and others wrong, but rather to what degree they "fit" and are useful and effective. Sandler concluded his comments by noting that his perspective may complicate the deliberations of the workshop, because it is misleading to consider interpretations, presented from any particular theoretical point of view, at a midpoint in the analysis. This important point concerning the technical implications of a pluralistic theoretical view was the subject of considerable discussion.

A number of the panelists (Drs. Arlow, Modell, Richardson, and Segal) espoused their individual evolutionary view of the process of the development of psychoanalytic theory while Drs. Levenson and Goldberg affirmed and emphasized the heuristic advantages of a revolutionary conception of the development of psychoanalytic models of the mind.

Arlow reminded the group that the Oedipus complex is a specific psychodynamic conception and not a model of the mind. Rather, the principles of unconscious dynamic determinism and unconscious conflict are at the base of his structural model of the mind. In regard to the "other schools," Arlow suggested that they have focused on underemphasized or obscure points within the structural hypothesis that require clarification. He enumerated four such points: (1) Where does the self fit in? (2) What do we really mean by an object? (3) What is the impact on current events of the experienced past? (4) Is transference really a replication of the past as such?

Segal stated that Melanie Klein's theoretical contributions were a development of the structural model that emphasized the origins of the superego and the ego. She suggested that the contributions of Klein, like those of Freud, excessively emphasized drive and deemphasized the influence of parental failures. Segal further proposed that Bion's conception of the mother as "container" of the baby's projective identifications has supplied a balance between the influence of the id on the one hand and the external world on the other. Bion's conception of the internalization of the mother as container into the developing ego is an important addition to a Kleinian theoretical understanding of optimal developmental progression from the paranoid–schizoid position. It is an addition so rich in its implications for understanding ego development and mode of therapeutic action that it influenced Segal to refer to her model as the Klein–Bion model.

In regard to her evolutionary pluralistic perspective, Segal noted that it is relatively easy to find similarities and build bridges when theory is discussed abstractly. However, she suggested that it was much more difficult to build bridges when one focused on issues of technique and on the question of timing and on what level to interpret. Segal noted that with a narcissistic patient she would interpret the narcissism as a projection onto the analyst of an identification employed by the patient as a defense against the painful affects of the dependent position. In contrast she noted that Kohut would not interpret the narcissism but would conceive of it as a developmental stage with which one should go along.

Dr. Richardson, from an evolutionary perspective, discussed Lacan's project and theoretical contributions as an attempt to lend a semiotic organizing perspective to our understanding of Freud's discovery of the dynamic unconscious. From that perspective he emphasized the unconscious as a language with a structure and analytic process as a discourse of language with the analyst's interventions conceived of as derived from his sensitivity to contiguity and context in the dyadic discourse.

Levenson repeatedly emphasized the potential disadvantages of excessive ecumenicism and the advantage of a revolutionary separatist perspective for the current development of psychoanalysis. He suggested that analysts should commit to specific models and work from their organizing perspectives, while reporting and discussing their results with colleagues working from alternate perspectives. Levenson reiterated that, for the analyst working from the interpersonal perspective, the "realm of investigation is only what goes on between people." He added that, "That is not to say there is not an internal experience." Levenson suggested that reasonable questions about a model of the mind are, "Is the position of the model internally consistent?" and "What are the heuristic consequences in therapy of holding a particular position?"

Goldberg, from his revolutionary vantage point differed with colleagues who espoused an evolutionary perspective. He stated, "In science development is usually not evolutionary in the way that Sandler, Rothstein, and Arlow suggest is happening with one theory assimilating new points of other theories." Goldberg added, "Psychoanalytic self psychology has grown to a point where it is clearly different from traditional conflict theory."

Charles Brenner, from a metatheoretical positivistic perspective clearly stated his unequivocal disagreement with the view that theoretical pluralism is something to affirm. He emphasized that theories do not make facts, rather they direct our attention to facts. He stated that, "When the psychoanalytic method is used by a competent therapist on an analyzable patient it provides the best data for constructing a theory. If you alter the method you will get altered data and if you derive a theory from that data it will be a less valuable theory. Similarly, if you work with an unanalyzable patient twice a week you will get altered data and if you base a theory on that data it will be a less valuable theory."

In striking substantive contrast to Sandler, but with a similar facilitating humor, Brenner emphasized that one theory was enough for him and affirmed his experience of finding his publicly stated theory quite satisfactory for his private deliberations. He recommended consistency between clinical work and theory and elaborated his disagreement with colleagues such as A. Freud, B. Lewin, and Sandler, who have suggested, for example, that there are advantages in employing the topographic theory when working with dreams and the structural theory when dealing with neurotic symptoms.

Goldberg criticized, as outmoded and old fashioned, Brenner's positivistic metatheory which suggests that there are facts to be found. Goldberg suggested the potential heuristic advantage in employing the philosopher of science Karl Popper's metatheory that proposes that theories do not direct one to facts that exist but rather create facts and designate what facts are. Goldberg noted that we are constantly evolving theory and that all that is possible is to say one has the best answer for the present time.

Modell differed with Brenner's view that the facts of psychoanalysis are derived from analyzable patients. Modell noted that this was not Freud's way; Schreber was not an analytic case and Dora was a failed case, yet both were profoundly important influences on Freud's evolving ideas. Modell proposed that we are working, at present, in a period of transition and suggested the advantage if not the necessity of entertaining the possibility of alternative ways of looking at things.

Finally, in regard to the controversies between the metatheoretical perspectives of positivism and pluralism, Rothstein suggested that pluralism is helpful in creating an ambience that facilitates communication between proponents of different psychoanalytic paradigms. However, he noted that pluralism is not a psychoanalytic theory. Karl Popper's version of pluralism is one theory of the history of science that enjoys considerable popularity today. Positivism, on the other hand, is not currently in vogue in that discipline. However, both models of the philosophy of science are in vogue as tertiary metatheoretical organizing perspectives in psychoanalysis. Rothstein suggested that it was quite conceivable that some evolved version of positivism might be in vogue during some future development of theory in the philosophy of science.

Before proceeding with a summary of the discussion of the clinical vignettes, it is worth reporting some interesting discussions of specific points of difference and agreement between various panelists.

In regard to Kleinian hypotheses concerning the infant's early fantasy life, Arlow emphasized the question of methodology. He asked, "By what method can you demonstrate the validity of reconstructions of the events of very early periods of life from what you experience in the transference?" Arlow suggested that beyond the methodologic question one can at best have only heuristic speculations. In relation to the question of deficit, it was interesting that both Arlow and Segal agreed that its consequences should be interpreted. Arlow emphasized his view that any deficit is involved in conflict. Segal noted that if the analyst does not interpret the events of the first two years of life their pathologic sequelae lead to parameters or nonanalytic responses.

Goldberg noted an interesting point of difference between Kohut's and Lacan's, and implicitly, Freud's vision of the world. Goldberg invoked the infant observational findings of Louis Sander to support Kohut's view that the child is basically joyful and fulfilled if nurtured in an affirmingly responsive selfobject milieu.

Goldberg inquired of Richardson concerning his understanding that Lacan conceives of the infant as entering a life characterized by resignation. Richardson agreed with Goldberg's reading of Lacan. He elaborated upon Lacan's view of the child as lacking. Lacan conceived of the child as torn from the mother and thereafter needing to mediate the resulting lack via the symbolic order. For Lacan, then, the desire to be derives from a lack and that lack is the basis of desire and of the interminable gap between signifier and signified.

Arlow and Modell disagreed in regard to the question of the potential heuristic advantage of thinking of different models' relationship to, and specificity for, certain groups of patients. Arlow stated that a model is a generalization about people not about specific groups of patients, and added that therapeutic applicability is not the central criterion for evaluating the efficacy of a model. Modell disagreed, and suggested that Freud's model evolved from the topographic theory to the structural hypothesis in response to clinical material. He added that in a similar fashion the workshop derived, in part, from interest in so-called narcissistic patients. Modell suggested that for patients like the one Arlow described who can free associate, the structural model is fine. But he suggested that a different model is advantageous for understanding patients who cannot free associate for years because their mistrust does not allow them to feel sufficiently safe in the analytic situation. For this kind of patient who presents with a problem in object relations, an object relations model is helpful. Modell conceived of the future attainment of an overriding model.

The theoretical discussions provided a rich background for exchanges concerning the clinical vignettes presented by the panelists. A question of untold importance that was not definitively answered was the influence of theory on process and outcome. Do different theories generate different responses, timing, interpretations, and processes or do all theories, sooner or later, some a bit better, some a bit worse in particular situations, allow analyst and patient to arrive at a similar end point?

Goldberg, from the perspective of the question, "Can self psychology add anything?" commented on Arlow and Levenson's cases. In relationship to Arlow's case Goldberg suggested that a self psychologist would find the analyst's impending vacation most important and would be sensitive to what the experience of the patient was in response to the loss of the support of the idealized omnipotent selfobject. In regard to Levenson's case, Goldberg noted that the self psychologist would suggest that the patient would not have acted out missing the hour to pursue an affair if there hadn't been a break in the self-selfobject transference. Goldberg reiterated that it is the sensitivity to the inevitable breaks in the selfobject transferences and their working through that is what psychoanalytic self psychology has added and is the essence of psychoanalysis for its practitioners.

Levenson, from the interpersonal perspective, would have wondered whether Arlow's patient was concerned about his analyst's health, and noted that he came to Dr. Arlow to obtain help so he would not kill himself, as his brother and perhaps his father had done.

Segal commented on Levenson's potentially self-revelatory countertransference interpretation. She stated, emphasizing the radically different technical implication deriving from their different theoretical points of view, "What I would never say to a patient is 'You're an attractive young man.' " She added, "It's a value judgment. . . . It is to say I find you attractive. . . . It is a fantastic communication. . . . I might say you're a young man." These comments led her to query, "Why did the patient make the analyst jealous? What was being acted out?"

Brenner commented on Levenson's vignette in a manner similar to Segal, emphasizing that different theories dictate different technical responses. He stated, "His interpersonal theory dictated the response 'How do you know I'm not jealous? You're an attractive young man. I'm middle aged. How do you know I'm not jealous?' " Brenner continued, "My conflict theory would influence me to think that Dr. Levenson's patient thought of Dr. Levenson as jealous; he became anxious and dealt with his anxiety by saying to himself, 'Oh that's crazy; Dr. Levenson couldn't be jealous of me.' " Brenner concluded, "I would have called attention to the fact that he was reassuring himself and that in fact he was frightened that Dr. Levenson was jealous of him."

Both Brenner and Segal were interested in interpreting Levenson's patient's frightening intrapsychic experience. Their differences involved psychodynamic conceptions of pathogenesis which would influence what Segal referred to as the level and timing of the interpretations.

Levenson responded to these comments by stressing that from his interpersonal organizing perspective acting out was defined as anything that makes the analyst anxious. He stressed that his aim was not to correct a distortion. Rather, his aim was to help his patient to understand that he felt something, and that feeling could evoke feelings in others, and that that was a basic event of live.

Modell, in the service of facilitating communication, suggested that the panelists were much too polite with each other. He emphasized that there were very real differences and they ought to be discussed. Toward that end he commented on Segal's patients and wondered if the computers and the motorcycle in the head were artifacts of Dr. Segal's technique which Modell characterized as "excessively early deep interpretations." In regard to his criticism of Segal's technique, he noted a similarity between his object relations perspective and self psychology in regard to early process. Both allow for the patient's creativity and both share a noninterpretive perspective toward early process. Modell stated: "I'd be aware that any interpretation I'd make early might be experienced as an intrusion."

In response to Modell, Segal defined a fundamental difference between the organizing perspective of her Klein–Bion model and that afforded by Winnicott's contributions. She noted that Winnicott sees the baby as a tabula rasa to be written upon by the mother's ministrations. Whatever goes wrong does so within the faults in the mother's "holding" which are repaired by the analyst's holding. She noted that Klein sees the baby, as

Freud did, as an active agent with inborn destructive and loving impulses.

In their final concluding remarks a number of the participants commented on the irrational elements in therapists' theoretical affinities.

Modell reminded his colleagues that all analysts present had been influenced by great teachers. He suggested that if we are not to become cultish and isolated in schools, we need to be able to be critical of our great teachers. Cooper noted that it was threatening to model exponents to consider their model, and implicitly its creator, as imperfect and in need of improving. In a related vein Sydney Pulver suggested that nothing helps uncertainty in the clinical situation so much as the illusion of possessing a correct model, and thereby knowing what is going on.

This book has provided a rich opportunity to study a diversity of work by sophisticated, experienced clinicians pursuing their efforts from a spectrum of organizing perspectives with radically different technical implications. Yet all participants work within a tradition that conceives of itself as analysis and each is deeply committed to that tradition. This book is, in addition, permeated by a feeling that while these differences exist and produce anxiety and uncertainty, they also provide an opportunity for research and communication between proponents of competing perspectives. In that vein Sandler concluded the workshop by speaking to the closed-minded tendency that paradigm affiliation sometimes engenders, asking all present to "try to listen to what other people are saying."

References

Arlow, J. (1969a), Unconscious fantasy and disturbances of conscious experience. *Psychoanal. Quart.*, 38:1–27.
—— (1969b), Fantasy, memory and reality testing. *Psychoanal. Quart.*, 38:28–51.
Balint, M. (1968), *The Basic Fault.* London: Tavistock.
Bion, W. R. (1957), Differentiation of the psychotic from the non-psychotic personalities. *Internat. J. Psycho-Anal.*, 38:266–275.
—— (1962), *Learning From Experience.* New York: Basic Books
—— (1970), *Attention and Interpretation.* New York: Basic Books.
Bowlby, J. (1969), *Attachment.* New York: Basic Books.
—— (1973), *Attachment and Loss*, Vol. II, *Separation Anxiety and Anger.* New York: Basic Books.
Breger, L. (1981), *Freud's Unfinished Journey.* London: Routledge & Kegan Paul, chapter 3.
Bruch, H. (1983), *William Alanson White Newsletter*, 17: #1 Winter 1982/83, 40th Anniversary issue.
Chatelaine, K. (1981), *The Formative Years: Harry Stack Sullivan.* Washington, D.C.: University Press of America, pp. 45–46.
Cooper, A.M. (unpublished), Psychoanalytic technique: one method or more. Presented to the Association for Psychoanalytic Medicine, Dec. 9, 1977.
—— (1983), Psychoanalytic inquiry and new knowledge. In *Reflections of Self Psychology*, ed. J.D. Lichtenberg and S. Kaplan. New Jersey: Analytic Press, pp. 19–34.
—— (1984), Psychoanalysis at one hundred: Beginnings of maturity. *J. Amer. Psychoanal. Assn.*, 32:245–267.
Crowley, R. (1984), Book review. *Amer. J. Ortho-Psychiat.* January. 54:1.
Eissler, K. R. (1953), The effect of the structure of the ego on psychoanalytic technique. *J. Am. Psa. Assn.*, 1:104–143.
Epstein, L., & Feiner, A. (1979), *Countertransference.* New York: Jason Aronson.
Erikson, E. (1954), The dream specimen of psychoanalysis. *J. Amer. Psychoanal. Assn.*, 2:5–55.
Fairbairn, W. R. D. (1952), *Psychoanalytic Studies of the Personality.* London: Tavistock.
Ferenczi, S. & Rank, O. (1922), *The Development of Psychoanalysis.* New York: Dover Publications, 1956.
Forrester, J. (1980), *Language and the Origins of Psychoanalysis.* New York: Columbia University Press.

Freud, A. (1936), *The Ego and the Mechanism of Defense*. New York: International Universities Press, 1948.

Freud, S. (1891), *On Aphasia*. New York: International Universities Press, 1953.

—— (1892–1899), Extracts from the Fliess papers. *Standard Edition*, 1:177–280. London: Hogarth Press, 1966.

—— (1895), Project for a scientific psychology. *Standard Edition*, 1:281–397. London: Hogarth Press, 1966.

—— (1900–1901) The Interpretation of Dreams. *Standard Edition*, vols. 4 & 5. London: Hogarth Press, 1953.

—— (1905), Fragment of an analysis of a case of hysteria. *Standard Edition*, 7:1–122. London: Hogarth Press, 1953.

—— (1914), On narcissism: An introduction. *Standard Edition*, 14:73–102. London: Hogarth Press, 1957.

—— (1920), Beyond the pleasure principle. *Standard Edition*, 18:7–64. London: Hogarth Press, 1955.

—— (1925), An autobiographical study. *Standard Edition*, 20:3–74. London: Hogarth Press, 1959.

—— (1925b), Negation. *Standard Edition*, 19:235–239. London: Hogarth Press, 1961.

—— (1937), Analysis terminable and interminable, *Standard Edition*, 23:216–253. London: Hogarth Press, 1964.

74—— (1940), An outline of psychoanalysis. *Standard Edition*, 23:144–207. London: Hogarth Press, 1964.

Gedo, J. (1979), *Beyond Interpretation*. New York: International Universities Press.

Gellner, E. (1974), *Legitimation of Belief*. Cambridge, London: Cambridge University Press.

Gill, J. (1983), The interpersonal paradigm and the degree of the therapist's involvement. *Contemp. Psychoanal.*, 19:2, 200.

Gill, M. (1982), *Analysis of Transference*, Vol. I. New York: International Universities Press, p. 13.

Goldberg, A. (1985), Translation between psychoanalytic theories. *The Annual of Psychoanalysis*, 12/13.

Greenberg, J., & Mitchell, S. (1983), *Object Relations in Psychoanalytic Theory*. Cambridge, Mass.: Harvard University Press.

Hesse, M. (1978), Theory and value in the social sciences. In: *Action and Interpretation*, ed. Christopher Hookway & Philip Petit. Cambridge/London: Cambridge University Press.

Hoffman, I. (1983), The patient as interpreter of the analyst's experience. *Contemp. Psychoanal.*, 19:3, 389–421.

Kernberg, O. (1975), *Borderline Conditions and Pathological Narcissism*. New York: Jason Aronson.

Klein, M. (1948), On the theory of anxiety and guilt.

—— (1952), Some theoretical conclusions regarding the emotional life of the infant, pp. 198–236. In: *Developments in Psycho-Analysis*, ed. Joan Riviere. London: Hogarth Press, 1952.

Kohut, H. (1977), *The Restoration of the Self*. New York: International Universities Press.

—— (1982), Introspection, empathy and the semi-circle of mental health. *Internat. J. Psycho-Anal.*, 63:395–407.

——— (1984), *How Does Psychoanalysis Cure?* ed. A. Goldberg & P. Stepansky. Chicago: University of Chicago Press.

Kuhn, T. S. (1962), *The Structure of Scientific Revolutions.* Chicago: The University of Chicago Press.

Lacan, J. (1954–1955), *Le Séminaire.* Vol. II, *Le moi dans la theorie de Freud et dans la technique de la psychanalyse,* ed. J. A. Miller. Paris: Editions du Seuil, 1978.

——— (1977), *Ecrits: A Selection,* trans. A. Sheridan. New York: W. W. Norton.

Laing, R. D. (1967), *The Politics of Experience.* New York: Pantheon Books.

Levenson, E. (1983), *The Ambiguity of Change.* New York: Basic Books.

Lipton, S. (1977), The advantages of Freud's technique as shown in his analysis of the rat man. *Internat. J. Psycho-Anal.,* 58:255–274.

Loewald, H. (1980), *Papers on Psychoanalysis.* New Haven, Conn.: Yale University Press.

McDougall, J. (1980), *Plea for a Measure of Abnormality.* New York: International Universities Press, pp. 213–246.

Mahler, M. S., Pine, F. & Bergman, A. (1975), *The Psychological Birth of the Human Infant.* New York: Basic Books.

Mehlman, R. D. (1976), Transference mobilization, transference resolution and narcissistic alliance. Paper presented to the Boston Psychoanalytic Society and Institute, 25 February 1976.

Menninger, K., & Holzman, P. (1958), *Theory of Psychoanalytic Technique.* New York: Basic Books.

Modell, A. (1965), On having the right to a life: An aspect of the superego's development. *Internat. J. Psycho-Anal.,* 46:323–333.

——— (1971), The origin of certain forms of pre-oedipal guilt and the implications for a psychoanalytic theory of affects. *Internat. J. Psycho-Anal.,* 52:337–346.

——— (1975), A narcissistic defense against affects and the illusion of self-sufficiency. *Internat. J. Psycho-Anal.,* 56:275–282.

——— (1976), "The holding environment" and the therapeutic action of psychoanalysis. *J. Amer. Psychoanal. Assn.,* 24:285–307.

——— (1984), *Psychoanalysis in a New Context.* New York: International Universities Press.

Ricoeur, P. (1970), *Freud and Philosophy.* New Haven/London: Yale University Press.

Rosen, V. (1967), Disorders of communications in psychoanalysis. *J. Amer. Psychoanal. Assn.,* 50:467–490.

Rosenfeld, H. (1952), Notes on the psycho-analysis of the superego conflict in an acute schizophrenic patient. *Internat. J. Psycho-Anal.,* 33:111–131.

Sandler, J. (1960), The background of safety. *Internat. J. Psycho-Anal.,* 41:352–356.

——— (1974), Psychological conflict and the structural model: Some clinical and theoretical implications. *Internat. J. Psycho-Anal.,* 55:53–62.

——— (1983), Reflections on some relations between psychoanalytic concepts and psychoanalytic practice. *Internat. J. Psycho-Anal.,* 64:35–45.

Sartre, J. P. (1953), *Existential Psychoanalysis.* New York: Philosophic Library.

Segal, H. (1964), *Introduction to the Work of Melanie Klein.* New York: Basic Books.

Sullivan, H. S. (1953), *The Interpersonal Theory of Psychiatry.* New York: W. W. Norton, p. 343.

—— (1956), *Clinical Studies in Psychiatry*. New York: W. W. Norton.

Treurniet, N. (1980), On the relation between concepts of the self and ego in Kohut's psychology of the self. *Internat. J. Psycho-Anal.*, 61:325–333.

Valéry, P. (1956), *An Anthology*, ed. J. J. Lawler, Bollinger series KLV. Princeton, N.J.: Princeton University Press, p. 49.

Wallerstein, R. (1983), Self psychology and "classical" psychoanalytic psychology: The nature of their relationship. In: *The Future of Psychoanalysis*, ed. A. Goldberg. New York: International Universities Press.

Winnicott, D. (1954), Metapsychological and clinical aspects of regression within the psychoanalytic set-up. In: *Collected Papers*. New York: Basic Books, 1958.

—— (1965), *The Maturational Processes and the Facilitating Environment*. New York: International Universities Press.

—— (1969), The use of an object. *Internat. J. Psycho-Anal.*, 50:711–716.

—— (1971), *Playing and Reality*. New York: Basic Books.

Name Index

Abraham, K., 11
Adler, A., 3, 11, 12
Arlow, J., 21–33, 116, 117, 120, 123, 124, 131, 134, 139, 141, 143, 144, 145

Balint, M., 85, 86, 98, 99
Benedict, R., 52
Bion, W.R., 37, 40, 41, 45, 46, 86–87, 94, 132, 140
Bowlby, J., 50, 89
Brecht, B., 52
Breger, L, 71
Brenner, C., 3, 121, 141, 142, 145, 146
Breuer, J., 3
Bridgeman, 51
Bruch, H., 66

Chatelaine, K., 55
Cooper, A.M., 2, 3, 5–20, 121, 122, 130, 134, 137, 147
Crowley, R., 52

Dewey, J., 51

Einstein, A., 52, 77
Eissler, K.R., 126
Epstein, L., 62
Erikson, E., 130, 138

Fairbairn, W.R.D., 12, 15, 53, 85, 86, 99, 126
Feiner, A., 62

Ferenczi, W., 15
Fliess, W., 109
Forrester, J., 109
Fromm, E., 52
Freud, A., 10, 22, 24, 142
Freud, S., 3, 6, 7, 8–9, 10, 11, 12, 13, 15, 16, 18, 21–22, 35, 36, 37, 39, 40, 44, 45, 50, 52, 53, 56, 59, 71, 76, 79, 88, 89, 93, 102, 103, 104, 105, 106, 109–115, 125, 130, 131, 134, 135, 137, 138, 140–144, 147

Gedo, J., 93
Gellner, E., 74
Gill, J., 62
Gill, M., 16, 56, 61
Goldberg, A., 69–84, 120, 125, 126, 133–135, 139, 141–145
Greenberg, J., 52, 66

Hartmann, H., 10
Hesse, M., 72
Hoffman, I., 61, 64
Holzman, P., 60
Horney, K., 52

Isaacs, Susan, 122

Jacobson, R., 103
James, W., 51
Jung, C., 3, 11, 12, 16

Kardiner, 12

153

Kernberg, O., 86, 99
Klein G., 6
Klein M., 12, 18, 35, 36, 38, 40, 45–47, 86, 87, 89, 131, 132, 138, 140, 146
Kohut, H., 12, 14–16, 18, 19, 57–60, 76, 98, 99, 125, 130, 132, 133, 135, 140, 143
Korzybski, 52
Kuhn, T.S., 3, 6, 53

Lacan, J., 16, 102–111, 126, 134, 143, 144
Laing, R.D., 51
Lebovici, S., 35
Levenson, E., 49–67, 137, 139, 141, 144–146
Levin, B., 142
Lévi-Strauss, 103, 104
Lifton, R., 62
Lipton, S., 88
Loewald, H., 91

McDougall, J., 94, 95
Mahler, M.S., 46, 131, 138
Mead, M., 52
Mehlman, R.D., 133
Menninger, K., 60
Meyer, A., 51
Michels, R., 3
Mitchell, S., 53, 66
Modell, A., 85–100, 120, 126, 133–135, 139, 142, 144, 146, 147

Newton, I., 108

Peirce, C., 51

Popper, K., 142, 143
Pulver, S., 3, 147

Rado, S., 12
Rank, O., 11, 12, 15
Richardson, W.J., 101–117, 126, 134, 139, 140, 143
Ricoeur, P., 74
Rosen, V., 23
Rosenfeld, H., 37
Rothstein, A., ix–x, 1–3, 129–135, 137, 141, 142, 143

Sander, L., 143
Sandler, J., 3, 89, 119–127, 137, 138, 139, 141, 142, 147, 151
Sapir, E., 52
Sartre, J.-P., 51, 151
de Saussure, F., 103
Schafer, R., 16
Segal, H., 35–47, 120, 125, 131, 132, 139, 140, 141, 143, 145, 146, 151
Sullivan, H.S., 14, 15, 16, 18, 49, 50, 51, 52, 53, 54, 55, 60, 62, 64–65, 66, 67, 125, 126, 130, 132, 133, 135, 151

Tausk, V., 8
Treurniet, N., 98, 152

Valéry, P., 49, 152

Wallerstein, R., 98, 152,
Wilder, B., 52
Winnicott, D., 12, 14, 53, 85, 86, 87, 88, 90, 92, 93, 94, 96, 97, 98, 99, 126, 133, 146, 152

Subject Index

Analyst's role, *see* Therapist's role
Antianalysands, 94
Anxiety
  about anxiety, 50
  excessive, 37
Anxiety dream, 119–120
Axis of combination, Lacanian, 104
Axis of selection, Lacanian, 104

Bad Me, 50–51
Bion model, 37, 40, 41, 45, 46; *see also*
  Klein-Bion model

Capacity to learn, 95, 96, 97
Clinical cases, 135
  anxiety dream, Sandler's, 119–120
  comments on each others', 144–146
  critique of clinical work, Sandler's,
    120
  Klein-Bion model, 41–45
  Object relations theory, 94–96
  structural hypothesis, 26–32
  Sullivanian/interpersonal model,
    57–60, 62–65
  treatment failure, 94–96
Clinical work; *see also* Technique/
    therapy/treatment
  psychoanalytic theory and, 121,
    123–124
  real theory behind, 123–124, 138
  structural hypothesis and, 24–25
Compromise formation, 25
Condensation, 134
Confidentiality, 31–32

Conflict, 21, 22, 138
  in human nature, 16
  preoedipal, 133
  psychology of deficiency states
    compared to, 98
  and self/object differentiation,
    91–92
  in self-psychology, 77–78
  and structural hypothesis, 21, 22,
    29–30, 30–31, 123, 124–125
  unconscious, 131
Consciousness, 25
Container and contained, 45–46
Countertransference, interpersonal
    nature of, 40, 60, 62, 65–67
Cultural anthropology, 103

Data of psychoanalysis, 49
Deficiency states, psychology of, 98
Dependency, 86
Depressive position, 46–47
Destructiveness, 94
Determinism, psychic, 8
Development
  preoedipal, 131–132
  of self-object differentiation, 90,
    91–92
  Sullivan on, 54–55
Developmental view, 14
Disciplinary matrix, 2; *see also* Para-
    digms
Displacement, 134
Dora case, 111–116, 142
Dreams, 23–24

155

Drive theories, self-psychology and, 83
Dying patient, 83

Ego
 Freud on, 106
 Lacan on, 106–107
Existential analysis, 12

Fact and theory, 134, 141–142
Fantasy
 concept of, 121–122
 infant's early, 143
 interpersonal model of, 49
 sources of, 9–10
Free association, 21, 22, 23
Freud, Sigmund, 3, 6, 7, 8–9, 10, 11, 12, 13, 15, 16, 18, 21–22, 35, 36, 37, 39, 40, 44, 45, 50, 52, 53, 56, 59, 71, 76, 79, 88, 89, 93, 102, 103, 104, 105, 106, 109, 110, 111, 112, 113, 114, 115, 125, 130, 131, 134, 135, 137, 138, 140, 141, 142, 143, 144, 147
 Adler, response to, 11
 on anxiety, 50
 attitude toward his own theories, 7–8
 Dora case, 111–116, 142
 on ego, 106
 on free association, 21–22
 intolerance of, 8
 Irma dream, 110
 Jung, response to, 11
 major shifts in, 9–10
 Rank, response to, 11
 Rat Man case, 88
 Schreber case, 142
Freudian theory
 challenges to, 11
 core of psychoanalysis, 6, 8–9
 interpersonal model vs, 52, 53–54
 Kleinian theory and, 35, 39–40
 Lacanian theory and, 109–111
 metapsychology of, 7–8, 10

opposing schools or movements, 11–12
 paradigms and revisions of, 6
 structural model of, see Structural hypothesis
 Sullivan on anxiety compared with, 50
Frustration in paranoid-schizoid position, 45

Genetic-developmental proposition, 9
Genetic viewpoint, 14
Good Me, 50–51
Guilt, 98–99

Hermeneutics, 16, 72, 73, 74
Human nature, 16

Individuation
 depressive position of Klein compared with Mahler on, 46–47
 guilt and, 99
Infant's early fantasy life, 143
Instincts/drives, 9–10, 89
 dual instinct theory, 10
 object relations theory and, 89
Internal dialogue, 23
Interpersonal (Sullivanian) model, 49–67, 125, 132–133, 141
 anxiety and, 50
 clinical cases, 57–60, 62–67
 countertransference in, 60, 62, 65–67
 development in, 54–55
 Freudian theory compared with, 52, 53–54
 influences on, 51–52
 languange and, 52
 needs and, 54, 133
 patient-therapist relationship in, 61–65
 treatment goal of, 55, 66
 unconscious in, 51
Irma dream, 110

Klein-Bion model, 35–47, 99, 140
on narcissism, 140
as structural and interpersonal model, 40
Winnicott's contributions to, 146–147
Kleinian model, 125, 127, see also Klein-Bion model
depressive position in, 38–39, 46–47
Freud's model compared with, 39–40
Freud's structural model and, 35
individuation and separation of Mahler and, 46–47
paranoid-schizoid position in, 36
projective identification, 36–38
two basic positions in, 36
Kohut's model, 98–100, 125–126; see also Self-psychology, psychoanalytic

Lacanian theory, 101–117, 126, 134, 140–141, 143–144
axis of combination and axis of selection in, 104
Dora case and, 111–116
Freud as patron of, 109–111
language in psychoanalysis and, 102–104
register of the imaginary in, 105–107
register of the real in, 105, 107–109
structural linguistics and, 103–104
structural theory and, 116–117
symbolic, 102–103
symbolic order, 104–105
symptom formation and, 111–112
naming in, 102, 108
therapeutic process and, 102
Language and psychoanalysis, 70–75; see also Lacanian theory
Lacanian theory and, 102–104
in origins of psychoanalysis, 109
Sullivan on, 52
Learn, capacity to, 95, 96, 97

Mature dependency, 86
Metaphor, 134
Metapsychology, Freud's, 7–8, 10, 110
Methodology and infant's early fantasy life, 143
Metonymy, 134
Models of mind, see also Psychoanalytic theories
characteristics of/model of models, 17–19
pluralism and, 41
Mother as container, 45–46, 140
Motivational system, Freud's, 8–9

Naming, Lacan on, 102, 108
Narcissistic patients, 19, 92, 93, 98–99, 140
object relations model and, 92, 93
Oedipus complex in, 98–99
Needs, Sullivan on, 54, 133
Not Me, 50–51

Object-relations theorists, 53
Object relations theory, 85–100, 126
clinical vignette, 94–96
contribution of various psychoanalysts to, 86
destructiveness in, 94
environmental trauma in, 87–88
four broad groups of, 99
guilt in, 98–99
how treatment works in, 92
importance of actual object in, 87
inner vs outer object in, 86–87
instincts and, 89
Kohut's self psychology compared with, 98–100
naricssistic patients and, 92, 93
safety vs Oedipal content in, 93
self/object differentiation in, 90, 91–92
self psychology compared with, 98–100, 140, 146
as special point of view, 88

spontaneity of self in, 93–94
symbolic equivalents and regression in, 90–91
therapeutic illusion in, 91–92
transference in, 89
two theories in, 86–87
Oedipus complex, 13–14, 131, 139
avoidable vs inevitable, 99
in narcissistic patients, 98–99
in object relations theory, 92, 93
Operationalism, 51–52

Paradigms, 5–20
definition of, 2, 6
Freudian theory and, 6
Paranoid-schizoid position, 36, 45
Parent-child relationship
mother as container, 45–46, 140
parent's role, 132
symbolic equivalents of, 90–91
Psychic determinism, 8
Patient population and theory, 16–17, 18, 135, 144
narcissistic, 19, 92, 93, 98–99, 140
object relations theory, 92, 93
Patient's mistrust, 133
Patient-therapist relationship
object relations theory on, 88–89
as reality, 61–65
Penis envy model, 79, 81
Philosophy of science, 142–143
comparing theories, 74–75
paradigms in, 2, 6
postempiricism, 72
Pleasure-unpleasure principle, 8–9
Pluralism, theoretical, 41, 141, 142–143
Positivistic metatheory, 141, 142–143
Pragmatism, 51
Preoedipal conflicts, 133
Preoedipal deficit, 133
Preoedipal development, 131–132
Projective identification, 36–38, 45–46
Psychoanalysis
aim/goal of, 93–94

as-if attitude in, 19
data of, 49
developmental view in, 14
genetic viewpoint in, 14
interpretive work during, 25
language and, see Language and psychoanalysis
theory of, see Psychoanalytic theory
triadic praxis in, 56, 66
unit of study in, 14–15
values and, 120–121
what patient already knows, 57–60
Psychoanalytic paradigms, see Paradigms
Psychoanalytic theory/theories
challenges to, 11
comparing/judging theories, 74–75
conclusions, 129–135
core of, 6, 8–9, 56–57
development of, 123, 135, 139
disciples vs dissenters in, 130
discussion of various, 119, 127, 137–147
enduring conceptual disputes in, 13
European vs American, 51–53
facts and, 134, 141–142
Freud's attitudes toward his own, 7–8
Freud's intolerance of other, 8
as hermeneutic vs scientific causal discipline, 16
institutionalization of, 130
irrational elements in therapists' affinities, 147
pluralism, 41, 141, 142–143
positivistic metatheory, 141, 142–143
psychoanalysis and, 71–72
psychoanalysts who bore from within, 12
public (explicit) and private (implicit) models/real theory behind clinical work, 123–124, 138

real differences between, 53
schools or movements, 11–12
science and, 16, 70–75, 142–143
scientific openness and, 12–13
specific patient populations and,
  see Patient population and theory

Rat Man, 88
Register of the imaginary, 105–107
Register of the real, 105, 107–109
Regression in analytic situation, 86,
  90

Schools or movements, 11–12
Schreber case, 142
Science and psychoanalysis, 16, 70–75,
  142–143
  hermeneutics and, 16, 72, 73, 74
  hermeneutics vs causal, 16
  postempiricist account of, 72
Seduction hypothesis, 9
Self psychology, psychoanalytic,
  69–84, 133–134, 141
  clinical examples of, 77–82
  conflict in, 77–78
  definition of, 75–76
  discussion of, 82–84
  drive theories and, 83
  introduction to, 69–75
  modeling of the mind and, 75–77
  object relations theory compared
    with, 98–100, 140, 146
  penis envy model and, 79, 81
  role of therapist in, 82
  selfobject in, 76–77, 83, 98
Selfobject, 76–77, 98
  concept of developmental line of,
    83
  transference and, 76
Self-object differentiation, 90
Self-selfobject model, 77
Self-selfobject transference, 77
Self system, 50
Silent analyst, model of, 15

Spontaneity of self, 93–94
Structural hypothesis, 10, 21–33
  clinical cases, 26–32
  conflicts and, 21, 22, 29–31,
    123–125
  in linguistic mode, 116–117
  summary of, 32–33
  technical position of analyst in,
    24–25
  underemphasized or obscure points
    within, 140
Structural linguistics, 103–104
Sullivanian model, see Interpersonal
  (Sullivanian) model
Superego, 37
Symbolic, Lacanian theory of, 102–103
Symbolic equivalents in Lacanian theory, 90–91
Symbolic order in Lacanian theory,
  104–105
Symptom formation in Lacanian theory, 111–112

Technique/therapy/treatment; see also
  Clinical work
  aim of, 55, 66, 93–94, 139
  failure of, clinical vignette, 94–96
  Lacanian theory on, 102
  models and, 41
  Object relations theory and, 92; see
    also Object relations theory
  principles of, 93–94
  for specific patient populations, 18,
    19; see also Patient populations
    and theory
  structural hypothesis and, 24–25
  therapist's role in, 15–16, 24–25,
    60–61, 82
Theory, psychoanalytic, see Psychoanalytic theory/theories
Therapeutic illusion, 91–92
Therapeutic process, Lacanian theory on, 102
Therapist's role, 15–16, 24–25, 60–61,
  82

function of therapist, 60–61
proper behavior of, 15–16
in self psychology, 82
silent therapist, 15
structural hypothesis and, 24–25
Transference, 62, 66–67
concept of, 122
interpersonal nature of, 40
Object relations theory on, 89
selfobject, 76
Transference-countertransference in Sullivanian theory, 55, 66–67

Transference neurosis in Object relations theory, 89
Transitional object, 98
Trauma in Object relations theory, 87–88
Treatment, see Technique/ therapy/ treatment

Unconscious in Sullivanian theory, 51

Values and psychoanalysis, 120–121